First Published-1999

Reprint 2006

ISBN 81-7141-484-2

Published by:
DISCOVERY PUBLISHING HOUSE
4831/24, Ansari Road, Prahlad Street,
Daryaganj, New Delhi-110 002 (*INDIA*)
Phone: 3279245
Fax: 91-11-3253475

Printed at:
Arora Offset Press, Delhi-92.

PREFACE

The need of having a sports series felt because today's situation of the world is not conducive to peace, all round there is destruction, despair, conflict and war; war if not between two nations then within the country itself. In a world where there are some 820 million people unemployed or under-employed, and where 86 million people are born every year, it is not surprising that one out of every four individuals lives in absolute poverty. The *Discovery Publishing House* by Publishing this series seeks to get positive response as—to means by which sports can promote and propagate peace and international cooperation. Sportsmen form a large identifiable cadre. We visualises a situation where a conscious efforts is made all over the world to train the sportspersons to spread the message of peace and international cooperation. Instead of peace keeping efforts through arms and army, the sportspersons may be used as soldiers of peace in a subtle manner. The effort is to make the realize the contribution of sports as a factor for sustainable development, peace keeping and international cooperation.

In developing countries, sports development cooperation is still in the need of justification and steadfast arguments. Many people ask the question "why invest in sports in developing countries for which water supply, health service and agriculture projects are much better suited? An apt reply to this question may be "for many of the people of a developing country,

Sports is the only 'Sweaty' Leisure-time activity. Sports represents a moment of joy in the midst of hard poverty-stricken and dirty everyday life. Doing sports even makes one's work go more smoothly the next day.

This series will be useful to the sports promoters, organisers, coaches and other persons related or interested in sports.

Editor

CONTENTS

1 INTRODUCTION

Table tennis techniques have changed considerably in the last fifty years. One needs only to read books about table tennis describing the scene in the late 1920s to envisage the majority of men playing with long trousers and pimpled rubber rackets and not really going beyond the stroke play of defence and forehand and backhand smashes. Although sponge rackets were being developed by John Jacques and Company as early as 1927, players had limited success with them. Before 1937 certain players used to combine the effects of the 'fingerspin' service and their sponge racket to produce some surprising results in leading competitions. Their services were almost unplayable and the rallies were usually very short. However, after 1937 the 'fingerspin' service was banned and rallies tended to become quite prolonged. By 1951 a few players who used sponge rackets were producing good results and by 1954 several Japanese players using sponge rackets were gaining world supremacy, even though Japan did not enter the World Championships until 1952. They had been using sponge rackets in internal competitions for the previous twenty years.

With the development of the sponge racket the whole game of table tennis has changed in character.

Although sponge rackets as we know them today have been on the scene for over two decades the quality of the rubber has changed, and the same degree of speed and spin could not have been achieved in the past. As competition has thrived in the last twenty years, coaches all over the world have developed more and more advanced skill techniques and tactics.

The sponge racket was found to be ideal for putting tremendous spin on the ball and when it was being established in world play a point was often won by the service or, if not, by the smash which was used as the follow-up stroke. In the 1950s there was the introduction of a new stroke. It was really an exaggerated topspin where there was a greater preparation, follow-through and wrist action. The ball was given a finer touch and the stroke was nearer to the vertical plane. The loop drive in its simpler form had arrived. It had most probably been first thought of because players were getting used to their opponent's services and were able to return them in such a position that the server could not follow-up with a smash. Another vicious stroke was needed which could easily win the point and the loop drive seemed the most effective. This stroke really led to the downfall of the totally defensive player. Before its introduction there had been many defensive players but they were just unable to control the greater amount of topspin and were becoming easy opposition for people whom they had previously beaten. This disheartened many defensive players and they retired. Others eventually found the control to cope with the spin, but the added advantage for the attackers with the sponge racket meant that very few major men's championships were ever won by defensive players.

Attacking players also had difficulties in coping with the player who could get his loop drive in first, but they eventually learnt to block the ball effectively. Even then the chance of a good return was always difficult to predict.

The Asian penhold players demonstrated the way to counteract this 'new weapon' and they did it quite simply by intense pressure from their own serve and service return so that they could prevent the opponent getting a good loop in during a rally. They then followed up with a hard smash against a lesser degree of spin. Naturally a few of them developed loop drives as well, but they mainly relied on quick thrusting movements in the mode of hard smashes and blocks. It was not until the early 1970s that the loop drive was to find its true value against the penhold style of game.

The sidespin loop was to become more widely used and the loop drive against any style of ball from the opponent was to become very dominant. This is not to say that players would loop all the returns, but if it was necessary they could do so. The European players were moving further away from the table and therefore giving themselves more time to position themselves for, the faster return ball. The European nations had been practising this style since about 1965 but it was not until the 1970s that results really began to show, The possibility of a takeover from Eastern tactical supremacy had been showing in places throughout the world since 1970, but the big day came in Nagoya (Japan) in 1971 when Stellan Bengtsson from Sweden won the World Singles Championships and many Europeans obtained good results., Eventually by 1973, in Sarajevo seven out of the eight quart·r finalists in the World Championships were Europeans, and the Men's Team Championships was won by Sweden. Although The People's Republic of China won the Swaythling Cup in Calcutta in 1975, two Europeans contested the Men's Singles final for the first time since 1953. In the 1975 final Istvan Jonyer of Hungary defeated Anton Stipancic of Yugoslavia.

The tactical reasons for these results are as follows: The new rubbers which were being produced gave much more spin and speed and the Europeans were able to stay further away from the table and so have more time available to play their strokes. Even their slow controlled strokes had sufficient top and/or sidespin on them to prevent the hard flat hitters from making outright winners. Penhold strokes gradually became blocks instead of smashes and the initiative had thus passed to the European style. Europeans merely played the heavy topspin game if they could not kill the ball from the return of service, or service, then waited for the block to be slightly weak in positioning. Then they finished it either by a smash or a fast loop drive, often with sidespin so that it 'left the opponent'. The sidespin/topspin players posed many problems to the 'blockers' because there was so much variation of speed, spin and direction. Recently in Europe this blocking game has become less effective and now players only block occasionally and try to play their own loop or smash. This results in players often looping each others' loops for long rallies and often at great distances from the table.

After the 1975 World Championships in Calcutta the Chinese were to establish themselves firmly as the leading table tennis nation in the world. During these championships one of their leading lady players, Ke Hsin-Ai, easily won most of her games in the team event. She was using a racket especially made in China, which had on one side a very thin layer of sponge and long thin pimples and on the other side a more conventional amount of rubber and sponge. Each side of the racket imparted a completely different type of spin on the ball. Because the racket surfaces were identical in colour and she kept turning the racket in her hand between strokes it was almost impossible to tell which side of the racket she was using and therefore interpreting the spin on the ball was very difficult.

Before the World Championships in Birmingham in 1977, the Chinese men's and women's teams produced players who were very skilful with these rackets and they easily beat the top European players. The European players never learnt to counteract successfully the variation of spin by 1977 and China easily won both team championships in Birmingham. The only player who really played well against the Chinese players was Mitsuru Kohno of Japan and he went on to win the World Singles title. There are different views as to why Kohno won the title and it is still uncertain if he was actually allowed to win, because the Chinese had always stressed that friendship was more important than always winning and China had already won the Men's Team Championship. However, Kohno did have more opportunity of playing the Chinese players than did the Europeans in the two years before Birmingham and the Japanese coaches instructed him to listen to the different sounds when the ball hit the two sides of the Chinese player's racket. He then interpreted these sounds into the amount of spin on the ball and therefore had more time to play his strokes than the players who waited for the ball to bounce. However, it should be noted that Kohno beat a Chinese player in the semifinal and final of the singles yet he never won a match against the Chinese team in the final of the team event!

Because of the utter confusion in the interpretation by most players of the spin on the ball, the International Table Tennis Federation have banned the rackets with excessively long pimples so the era of these players may be over but that of China will not be, as they have many players who can play with conventional rackets and still beat most of the leading players in the world.

If one ignores the tactics of the players who used the long pimpled rackets one can summarise by stating that modern tactics today are:

1. Serve so that the other person is made to do what you want him to do. In practice you should have become used to countering every variation of return from your own services.
2. Follow-up if possible with a loop drive or smash or push the ball back short. A long heavy backspin push can be effective against a penhold player who does not use the loop drive.
3. When receiving serve ensure that you try to impart heavy topspin on any long serve: push or flick the return of the short service, short, or to an awkward position for the opponent, so your follow-up stroke can be an effective attacking stroke. In international-matches many points are won before the ball has crossed the net five times.

Review of successful countries

Men's teams

The People's Republic of China: Table tennis is the national sport in this country and there are, over one million players. The overall standard is extremely high and their coaching scheme is second to none. Their coaches have carefully studied all the leading players in all other countries and after analysing their weaknesses they have developed players with different styles so that they can oppose foreigners and know they will have a good chance of winning.

In the World Championships in Birmingham they included Kuo Yao Hua,, a penhold looping player, Li Chen-Shih, a fast flat hitting and blocking penhold player, and *Liang Ke Liang, a* shake hands grip defensive *player who also* had an excellent array of attacking strokes. All their players are extremely fit and have superb footwork. They are very good at following up their excellent services although there has been some criticism of their services because they sometimes impart spin on the ball during the 'throw up'.

Japan: The Japanese have continually gained honours in World Championships for the last twenty years., Table tennis is very popular in their universities and it is organised on a similar basis to collegiate sports in the United States of America. Many of their previous international players coach within the university system and they are all very dedicated in their work. Like the Chinese players, most of them use the penhold grip but nearly all of them prefer to use speed rather than excessive spin on their strokes.

Mitsuru Kohno, their current World Champion, concentrates on trying to play the ball at an early contact point and he obtains extreme angles when playing the ball. Unlike most European players he hits the ball very flat. The Japanese have yet to develop a really good looping player, either with the conventional shake hands grip or the penhold grip. They do have an excellent defensive player in Norio Takashima and he is a very valuable member of the team because his inclusion provides a variation of style to the rest of the team.

Sweden: Unlike the Chinese and Japanese, the Swedes seem to concentrate on producing players with one particular style of game and then they try to ensure that techniques are developed within the individual to counter all opponents. All their players have a good variation of services, mainly short with all aspects of sidespin, backspin and topspin combinations.

Their best players, especially Stellan Ben tsson and Kjell Johansson, have very consistent backhand counter attacks that do not have excessive spin but sufficient speed and excellent angles to create for the opponent difficulties in obtaining forehand domination. This allows them time to establish attacking domination with their backhand or forehand. They play many strokes about three feet from the table edge, between the backhand corner and centre of the table. They have excellent control of blocking the loop and can vary the block with sidespin or topspin. They usually prefer blocking if someone does get in with a loop, but they are quite capable of either smashing the loop with their forehand or moving back slightly and looping the loop, usually with more topspin than sidespin.

Yugoslavia: The coaching system in this country is similar to Sweden in that they tend to concentrate on coaching one style, but this style is different. In Dragutin Surbek and Anton Stipancic the Yugoslavs have a pair of player, as outstanding as Bengtsson and Johansson of Sweden. Surbek tends to dominate the, table with forehand strokes whereas Stipancic uses his backhand more often. Whenever possible, both of these players tend to impart topspin on the ball. They both have 'excellent touch' and if they cannot loop a service, they return the bill so that the opponent cannot play a devastating attacking stroke, then they get their loop drives into the rally. Surbek very rarely uses his backhand but concentrates on using his fitness to dominate with forehand loop drives. Stipancic is not as fit but he has wonderful control and imparts tremendous topspin and sidespin variation with both backhand and forehand. When receiving a loop drive they tend to stand further away from the table than the two Swedes and they play a loop return with both sidespin and topspin.

Hungary: After 1975 when Istvan Jonyer became the World Men's Singles Champion and the Men's Doubles Champion with his team-mate Gabor Gergely, the Hungarian National Teams were beset with injuries to their leading players. However, in the 1978 European Championships in Duisburg, West Germany, all the Hungarian players performed superbly and their men and women appeared in all seven finals.

Their men players won the team title, beating England 5-3 in the final, while in the Men's Singles event four of their players reached the quarter finals: Gabor Gergely. Istvan Jonyer, Tibor Kreisz and Tibor

Klampar. The latter lost to Desmond Douglas, but the other three players reached the semi-finals and Gergely defeated Jonyer in the final. Gergely also won the Men's Doubles in partnership with Milan Orlowski and Klarnpar and Gabriella Szabo lost in the Mixed Doubles final.

The National team and the most promising players in the provinces of the country are coached in Budapest, under, the guidance of their National Coach, Zoltan Berczik. The players are financially supported by the state and each player practises and performs physical training for approximately five hours per day.

The majority of their men players try to dominate their matches by using their forehand and backhand loop drives. Their forehand loop drives are very long strokes that impart tremendous amounts of topspin and sidespin upon the ball. Their backhand loop drives are also long strokes and they use this stroke more effectively than players from any other nation. If necessary they will allow the opponent to loop drive the ball and then they will loop the loop, a technique at which they excel.

Previous Hungarian teams have included some excellent defensive players. Kreisz, a promising yet not outstanding junior player in 1975, has now, become one of the best defensive players in the world.

Women's teams

The People's Republic of China: Like the men's team the women's team is very strong in its depth of table tennis talent. They have counter attacking, loop driving and defensive players, all of whom are quite capable of beating most players in the world. The 1975 and 1977

World Championships produced a Chinese victory in the Women's Team Event and their leading player, Chang Li, twice reached the final of the Womens Singles before losing to Pak Yung Sun of North Korea on each occasion. There are still many doubts as to whether the finals in 1975 and in 1977 were friendship games. As previously stated Ke Hsin-Ai caused havoc with her awkward blocking game and the unusual rubber on her racket. Chu Hsiang Yun has an excellent defensive game and her variety of backspin is very difficult to detect on her backhand strokes.

South Korea: The South Korean women's team have a fine record. In 1973, they won the World Championships Team Event and they finished runners-up to China in 1975 and 1977.

Most of their attacking players use a penhold grip but they have good defensive players who use the shake hands grip. Ailesa Lee is their best attacking player but as well as an excellent 'up to the table' game she has the exceptional ability to topspin lob very well when playing well away from the table. Chung Hyun Sook has a fine defensive game and her superb fitness allows her to move gracefully about the table. The variation of spin on her defensive strokes often confuses her opponents and this results in their making errors or setting the ball up in such a position that she can use forehand smash.

Hungary: Like their men counterparts the top lady players have missed many of the leading tournaments over the past few years because of injuries.

Judit Magos, Beatrix Kishazi and Gabriella Szabo easily won the European Team Championships in

Duisburg. Magos beat Jill Hammersley (England) in the final of the Women's Singles and she lost in the finals of the Women's Doubles partnered by Szabo. These players have contrasting styles of play and none is similar to the Hungarian men. Magos uses an unorthodox penhold grip and like most penhold grip players she has a good combination of forehand strokes. Kishazi has an excellent defensive game and Szabo has a good counter attacking and loop drive game.

'In the 1979 World Table Tennis Championships in Pyongyang, North Korea, the People's Republic of China retained the right to consider itself the leading nation in the world when their players captured four of the seven titles. In the Mixed Doubles and Women's Doubles Finals all the players were from the People's Republic of China, the only final in which they were not represented was in the Men's Doubles. The Chinese women players won all their events, but one of the major surprises of the championships was that their men failed to win the Men's Team Event or the Men's Singles. Seiji Ono, a left-handed attacking player, retained the Men's Singles title for Japan when he defeated Kuo Yao Hua of China, in an ill-fated final in which the latter was forced to retire with a torn hamstring. The Hungarian Men's Team, the 1978 European Champions, played superbly and probably surprised even themselves when they crushed the People's Republic of China 51 in the Men's Team Event final. This very impressive victory will no doubt create a great deal of interest for players, coaches and spectators alike as to what style of play will be the most effective in the future.

If you become hooked on table tennis, it won't be long before the words' ping pong' make you shudder.

Table tennis has come a long way from its genteel origins in the late nineteenth century as a descendant of lawn tennis. To begin with, it seems to have been largely a home-made pastime favoured by university students, The first patent for the game was registered in 1891 by Charles Barter of Gloucestershire, and about the same time a gentleman called James Gibb—who was a founder member of the Amateur Athletics Association brought some toy celluloid balls back from a trip to America which he quickly introduced as an alternative to the cork or rubber balls then being used. This move met with immediate success and several manufacturers started to market equipment under an assortment of names such as 'Gossima', 'Whiff Waff' and 'Flim Flam', even 'Table Tennis'.

When hollow, vellum-covered rackets were introduced, the dreaded moniker 'ping pong' was born, derived from the 'ping' sound which occurred when bat met ball, and the pong' that resulted as it bounced on the table. And it was Mr Gibb again who suggested to manufacturers John Jaques Ltd that this would be a catching title for their sets of bat, ball and net.

The craze caught on, and as early as 1901 tournaments were being organized with entries of 300 and over and prize-money of up to £25. The Ping Pong Association was formed, thankfully to be renamed The Table Tennis Association some time later in 1922.

In 1902 a visiting Japanese professor took the game back to the land of the rising sun where he introduced it to university students. Shortly after, a

British salesman—Edward Shires—introduced it to the people of Vienna and Budapest and the seeds were sown for a sport which now enjoys popular appeal in virtually every country in the world.

Back in Britain, table tennis had also begun to spread outside the distinctly middle-class confines of London and leagues sprang up in provincial towns as far apart as Plymouth and Sunderland. In 1922, an All England Club was formed which boasted such luminaries as Jack Hobbs the cricketer, and other famous names of the time from the world of sport. The *Daily Mirror* sponsored a nationwide tournament which attracted 40,000 competitors. Table tennis was firmly on the map and on 24 April 1927 the English Table Tennis Association came into being, under the chairmanship and direction of the late Ivor Montague, son of Lord Swaythling. Montague was not only to become the architect of modern-day table tennis, but he also achieved critical acclaim as both a film producer and director, At the time, the ETTA had a membership of nineteen leagues, it now has over 300, with around 75,000 registered players.

The first World Championships were held in 1927 and were won by a Hungarian, Dr Jacobi. Apart from the famous Fred Perry redressing the balance for England in 1929, this was to be the start of an unprecedented run of success for the Hungarians who dominated the game throughout the Thirties. Their team was led by the legendary Victor Barna, whose skill and inspiration did so much to elevate the game into becoming a sport to be taken seriously.

The 1950s saw the game turned upside down by the arrival of the 'sponge' or 'sandwich rubber', the revolutionary new material for bats which hitherto had been relatively simple affairs with a universal thin covering of pimpled rubber. Until this time, spin had played only a minor part in a game that had been dominated by the defensive style of play. But these new weapons, introduced by the Japanese, had the capacity to move the ball around in an almost magical way. The ITTF, the game's ruling body, was quick to legislate in a bid to control this new development, seen in some quarters as equipping players with an unfair advantage.

The thickness of the sponge and rubber sandwich' was controlled and remains so to this day. But the nature of the game had been changed, establishing the fast attacking speed-and-spin style of our current champions.

Today, the sport both in England and abroad stands strong and is growing year by year. The culmination of this has been its recognition as an Olympic sport, being featured for the first time in the 1988 Games in Seoul. Television coverage of the men's singles final attracted an amazing worldwide audience of two billion! In China, the game is played by literally millions, in school, at work, in the park, at the roadside. Their leading Players are regarded as national heroes with pop star' status.

Although in England we still have some way to go before table tennis overtakes games such as soccer as 'the national pastime', the picture is nevertheless an encouraging one. With players of proven world-class ability such as Desmond Douglas, Alan Cooke and Carl Prean, we have everything to look forward to. Backed by professional organization, a thriving

National Coaching Scheme, an expanding Schools' Association and a lucrative long-term sponsorship with the Leeds Permanent Building Society, the transition from minor to major sport is long overdue. Increasing TV and media coverage means that more people are taking up this fascinating game every day.

2

EQUIPMENT

One of the boasts made by table tennis experts is that the game can be played virtually anywhere. Unlike a tennis court, a table tennis table is portable and adaptable and can be moved in a matter of minutes from one location to the next. In many ways, however, its profile as a dynamic sport has suffered because of this very adaptability. More often than not, if the best facilities are required by other sports, table tennis tables tend to be shifted into an adjacent anteroom hidden from view. This is always disappointing as not only is the game losing valuable opportunities to create an impact and attract newcomers, but also it rarely does the players any favours as lighting is likely to be poor, the floor uneven or the space restricted. Therefore, the first consideration is to ensure that you have a suitable environment in which to play. Make sure that the lighting is adequate and visibility is even; that the floor gives good grip and lets the table sit evenly; that there is sufficient runback behind the tables and enough space between them to prevent the players from bumping into one another and injuring themselves.

Tables

Table tennis tables are either foldaway or the standard

static type, each of which have their advantages and disadvantages. The one you choose will very much depend on the situation in which the game is going to be played and the general standard of player who will be using it. The foldaway is easy to move as it sits as a complete unit on an undercarriage of wheels which detracts when the table is not in use. Furthermore, it takes only a matter of seconds to make ready for play. This type of table is ideal for beginners and with a little supervision can be erected by the youngest of players.

The static or standard table is a much more solid affair and once assembled gives a truer and more consistent bounce than the foldaway. For this reason, it tends to be preferred by more experienced players of league standard and above. Although it consists of two separate halves, the drawback is that table is awkward and heavy to handle and move around.

Choosing a bat

The commercial success of sports equipment manufacturers and retailers in recent years has been to bestow table tennis bats with an aura of magic and mythology. The range now available is massive and is compounded by the trend to have a bat 'made to measure', with a choice of the blade and two rubber surfaces which cover it. There are a number of detailed and complex laws set down by the International Table Tennis Federation (ITTF), the governing body of the sport, which regulates the design of table tennis bats. Each side of the bat should be clearly different in colour and the rubber should be stamped with the ITTF logo of approval. Virtually all manufacturers comply with the required legal specification, so the danger of buying an illegal weapon is now very remote.

As far as the beginner is concerned, the real danger lies in being tricked into spending a fortune and ending up with an expensive item which requires a high level of skill, touch and experience to use to full effect. Advise a beginner when selecting a bat to make sure that it is the 'all round' type. Careful inspection will usually reveal these very words stamped on the rubber. Ideally, it should be the reverse 'sandwich' type in which the pimples of the outer layer face inwards and are joined to the sponge layer. This sponge layer should preferably be no more than one and a half millimetres thick. If it is any thicker than this, the ability to control the ball will be made noticeably more difficult.

Bearing in mind that control is the most important factor for a beginner, it follows that similar attention should also be paid to the choice of blade. Firstly, make sure that the handle is comfortable so that it feels like a natural extension of the hand itself. Secondly, bearing in mind that the type of wood and number of ply affects the speed characteristic of the bat, a blade of five ply medium hardwood is ideal for beginners.

As a player becomes more experienced and proficient, the choice of bat becomes more significant but, nevertheless, the following ground rules still apply:

- The thicker the wood, the faster the bat
- The thicker and harder the rubber, the faster the bat
- The greater the 'grip characteristic of the rubber, the more spin can be imparted.

A bat of the 'all round' variety is relatively inexpensive and there is no reason why the blade cannot be recovered at a later stage. All rubber ultimately loses its grip on the ball and becomes stale and smooth. Equally, once the player has acquired a sound level of control, a good technique and a degree of skill, he may need to add more pace and spin to the game and a more sophisticated type of rubber may become necessary.

There is always a danger, though, that too much attention can be focused on the various characteristics and properties of the bat and not enough on good technique. Table tennis players are notorious for blaming their misfortune on their bats but it is always the bad workman who blames his tools.

Balls

There are two types of table tennis ball, plastic and celluloid. Although the plastic ones are the most durable, they are less common nowadays and, indeed, less popular among experienced players. The quality of the ball is determined by the star rating conferred on it by the ITTF, with three stars representing the best and most consistent on the market. The one and two-star balls may be suitable for practice purposes, but are rarely used in any formally organized competition.

Clothing and footwear

It's all too tempting with a sport such as ours to say that all you need are gym shoes and a bat. Clearly, we do not want to turn away anyone who wants to join in and discover the game, but at the same time, we should also be wary of conveying a sloppy image. This is, after all, a sport in the truest sense and when played at a high level, is physically demanding and very athletic. Even with a group of beginners, there is a lot to be said for encouraging a basic uniform of white gym shoes, white socks, dark shorts and T-shirt. None of these items should break the bank. Discourage the wearing of white or light-coloured shorts and shirts as light-coloured clothing runs the risk of being deemed contrary to the laws governing clothing. Most lightweight training shoes will be suitable as long as they give good adhesion to the floor and, if possible, support around the instep part of the foot.

If players take care of table tennis equipment, money can be saved, health maintained and performance will not be affected by external variables. So often neglect, laziness and carelessness lead to ruination of clothing, rackets, balls, tables and nets.

With clothing, a few principles should always be remembered. Plimsolls should be kept clean both for appearance's sake and prevention of perspiration bacteria rotting the material. It is essential that on completion of a day's play plimsolls are not just thrown away into a cupboard until the next time they are to be used. Always leave plimsolls well away from warm radiators or the resulting odour could be rather bad. Try to leave them in a place where fresh air circulates. Before wearing them again ensure that they are dusted down with a suitable powder or anti-perspirant. Many players often wear their plimsolls without any idea of the tread left on the soles'

They turn up at a tournament and find the floor is a little slippery. They have less friction with the floor and consequently their movement suffers as well as, or along with, their performance. This neglect of simple inspection could prove very costly in a critical game. It is very important that a player's footwear is comfortable. If the shoes are either too tight or too slack, footwork could easily be retarded. Plimsolls should offer good support, but they should also be light in weight. Excess weight means that more energy has to be expended on movement, even though the excess weight may be very slight.

If socks are worn for a second time, without being washed, bacteria will be present and this can irritate the skin and cause nasty rashes, such as Athlete's Foot. This can be very painful and can lead to distress in movement. Socks worn one day, or for any period of time should never be put on again until washed. Wear clean socks every day and after every training session or match. Thick cotton socks are usually better suited to table tennis than nylon ones.

Change underclothes as frequently as is convenient: preferably daily but unfailingly if worn during exercise, training or matches. Most sportsmen today wear a jockstrap and they are normally very comfortable. Try to avoid wearing the same table tennis clothes without their being washed. This applies especially to shorts. Wash in soap, not with chemical detergents. Rinse very thoroughly and dry slowly and at moderate temperatures—never in front of a fire or on a radiator. Comfort is also an important aspect of table tennis shorts. If shorts are too tight and retard movement in any particular direction then they are no good to that particular individual. They should not, however, be too slack or they will continually cause distraction to the player.

Shirts should be changed regularly. Often in a game one can perspire profusely and even after drying oneself and placing the shirt back on the body, perspiration can still occur. This is due to the body heat not dropping sufficiently. A shirt saturated in sweat should be replaced by another; otherwise the likelihood of catching cold is quite considerable, especially if the sweat is drying on the body in cold surroundings. Also shirts, like shorts, retain sweat which harbours infective bacteria. It is also advisable to put on your tracksuit as soon as a match has finished. This will prevent the heat of the body from coming into direct contact with the cold air. The actual air pockets between the tracksuit and skin will cause a type of extra blanket where the heat is trapped. It is also good to warm-up before a game with a tracksuit kept on. The body muscles will be 'warmed up' more quickly so that on starting the game a player will feel 'ready to go' from the first point.

In modern table tennis care of the racket is more important now than it has ever been before, Attacking players who rely on spin and speed in their play should change the rubber on their racket after about 60 hours of actual play. Within that time the ball has most probably made contact with the racket over half a million times, so it is quite understandable that the rubber should have lost some of its spring and taction. It often amazes me how players play year after year without changing their rubber and then they wonder why they do not obtain much speed and spin on the ball. It is essential to keep the racket in a dry place so that no water can actually soak into the wood and produce a warping effect. Rackets should be kept well away from really hot places like warm radiators or the rubber is likely to be seriously damaged. Before playing a game, ensure that the surface of the racket is free from dirt, grease or any other material that may cause the ball not to make proper contact. Methylated spirits on a clean handkerchief is usually quite adequate for removing most unwanted particles from the racket. Be very careful not to use a towel or material which sheds its fibres easily, otherwise the condition of the racket will not be improved. At the completion of the game, always place the racket in a good cover so it will be prevented from gathering dirt. Remember that during the previous game it will have collected particles of dirt from the ball which it in turn obtained from the floor, so clean the racket before playing the next match. When renewing the rubber, use a glue which will allow easy removal but still adhere quite adequately.

Table tennis balls also need to be carefully looked after. Quite a few Players find a variety of faults with different balls but if they like one they want to keep it in its original condition. If you are one of those players remember to place the ball in a solid type of cylindrical container which has a diameter just bigger than that of the ball. Many boxes of balls are too easily susceptible to external pressures. Always be very careful not to store balls in places of unusually high temperatures or the 'roundness' may be affected by the heat.

Table tennis tables are very expensive pieces of equipment, but if they are carefully looked after they can last for decades. Neglect a table and you will worth spending a little extra on buying a piece of rolling equipment like a roller skate so that the table edge can be placed on it and then conveniently rolled edge can be placed on it and then conveniently rolled to a safe storage area. Many tables now have wheels fitted into the centre edges of the table. In actual storage always place the centre edges of the table towards the floor with the surfaces together and use pieces of polystyrene as supports. Excess dirt particles should always be removed before a game so that there is no chance of an unusual bounce or the dirt being transferred to the ball and subsequently onto the racket. It goes without saying that one should never hit the table surface with the racket.

In table tennis, as in any other sport, a player will have to solve many problems before he reaches a high level of attainment. A major problem is that of using the most suitable racket for his style of game and also for the standard of play that he has attained. When the table tennis enthusiast purchases the monthly *Table Tennis News* or walks into a sports shop with the intention of buying a table tennis racket, he is usually uncertain about which blade or sandwich rubber he should use. Often the manufacturer's guidelines on the performance of each racket, sandwich rubber or blade are insufficient because they do not take into consideration the playing standard of the individual. This chapter is intended to explain the meaning *of* the speed and control of the blade and the speed, control and spin of the sandwich rubber.

During the World Championships In Calcutta in 1975 and in Birmingham in 1977, there were many players who were unhappy about the texture and thickness of the sponge and rubber on their opponents' rackets, and they felt they were at an unfair disadvantage during their matches. Many of the points were of a very short duration because the players were unable to assess what type of spin was on the ball, and they made mistakes very early in the rally. Many officials and players began to think that the texture of the sandwich rubber was winning the game rather than the skill of the player, so the International Table Tennis Federation made changes in the laws regarding the racket and these laws came into effect on 1 January 1978.

With these laws clearly understood a player can at least make sure that he does not buy an illegal racket. The blade consists of layers of plywood laminated together and as there is nothing stated in the laws limiting the thickness of the wood there can be as many layers as a player desires. Obviously he should take into consideration whether he likes a heavy or a light racket, before deciding on the thickness of the blade. If the racket is too light then he may note that he does not obtain a good sense of touch with the ball, whereas if the racket is too heavy he will have to consider that the arm is having to perform unnecessary work in moving a heavier rather than a lighter racket.

Different manufacturers produce a wide variety of blades, usually within a thickness range of three to seven layers of ply. These layers of ply vary in thickness and the quality of the wood can also vary from manufacturer to manufacturer, and from one range of racket to another. The difference in the quality of the wood and the thickness and number of layers of ply will affect the performance of the blade in relation to speed and control. Through past experiences of playing with various blades, the increased hardness of the ply, and the more layers of ply in the blade, will increase the speed and decrease the control of the racket in play; whereas the decreased hardness of the ply, and the fewer the layers of ply, will decrease the speed and assist the control of the racket in play.

When selecting a blade, a player should carefully consider the design of the handle. There are various types of handle in terms of length, thickness, width and weight and usually they are designed in one of the following shapes. There is no 'ideal' handle because players may hold the racket differently and hands vary in size. The important point to remember is to have a handle which feels comfortable in your hand during a game. Some people perspire very easily and if the perspiration contacts the racket handle then the racket could slip out, or alter its position in the hand during the execution of a stroke. Another solution is to sandpaper a varnished handle or to try to purchase a racket without a varnished handle.

An important part of the blade is the shoulder, that is, the meeting point of the handle and the main area of the blade. Blades have different sizes and shapes in the shoulder area, and not all blades may suit a particular style of grip. The two extremes of design of the shoulder area of the blade.

If a player prefers to grip the racket with the index finger completely on the main area of the blade he may feel discomfort in the area of the hand between the thumb and the index finger if he uses a grip.. Some players prefer not to have the whole of the index finger on the blade because they want to play strokes requiring great flexibility in the wrist joint; therefore they may want to play with a blade.

The sponge on a racket can vary in colour, thickness and quality. The sponge assists the rubber and blade in determining the speed with which the ball will be returned by the opponent. If the quality of the sponge is held constant then the thickness will determine the amount of control and speed it will possess. Usually, the thicker the sponge then the faster the speed but the less the control.

There are various kinds of rubbers that are manufactured throughout the world and thousands of pounds have been spent on developing the texture of the products. The names of these rubbers can be bewildering: Tackiness Drive, Tackiness Chop, Grass Attack, Grass Defence, Curl, Magnet, Super Flash, Bolt, Spectol, Knuckle, Cutman, Spin Ace, Tornado-Tic-Tac. etc. The novice table tennis player most probably, thinks he is buying a type of secret weapon. Basically, they have all been specially refined to give their own variation of speed and a frictional coefficient. To assess the qualities of each rubber, a scale has to be devised to evaluate speed, spin and control. If it is stated that a rubber has a great speed, it will mean that the ball will be catapulted off the rubber very quickly. The contact time between the ball and rubber is very small so there will be little opportunity to impart heavy spin upon the ball. It therefore follows that a pimpled rubber which has less surface area touching the ball upon contact cannot produce the same amount of spin per unit of time as a reversed rubber. If the rubber is very fast, then it will allow little control. During a 'lifetime', its catapult effect will be diminished, control will be increased and the maximum amount of spin that can be imparted upon the ball will be reduced.

There are numerous sandwich rubbers being produced at the moment that are designed to counter the spin and speed on the ball and they have a very low frictional coefficient. These rubbers usually provide excellent control but little spin or speed. If a player uses a racket with one of these sandwich rubbers then the techniques of certain strokes will have to be slightly altered to counter the spin and speed imparted on the ball by the opponent. These techniques will have to be mastered by improvising stroke play accordingly. The anti-topspin rubbers, the name by which these rubbers can be collectively described, can be pimpled or reversed sandwich rubber. The texture of the rubber and the sponge and more recently the length and thickness of the pimples have caused great confusion to many players. The frictional coefficient of the rubber was so low that the spin on the oncoming ball was completely different to that which the attacking player had been used to. When a player observed a certain stroke being played by the opponent he reacted by playing a 'conditioned' stroke. However, the amount and often the type of spin on the ball were miscalculated, therefore the stroke that was played usually resulted in the point being lost.

To add further to the player's confusion, opponents began to play with a sandwich rubber on one side of the racket that produced a great amount of spin and speed and used an anti-topspin sandwich rubber on the opposite side. The sandwich rubbers were exactly the same colour so detecting which side of the racket they were using was very difficult, especially since players kept changing the racket around in their hand below the height of the table.

Usually these players would serve, push or defend until the opponent misread the spin on the ball and if they had not won the point they would smash the high returned ball with their side of the racket with the sandwich rubber that produced speed and spin. What was happening when the different spins were making contact with the anti-topspin sandwich rubbers was quite simple. As stated earlier, the rubber produced very little spin or speed so really the opponent was virtually 'playing against himself'. If he imparted little spin on the ball he received very little, and if he imparted a vast amount of topspin or backspin then heavy spin was returned to him.

From all the above information a player must try and decide what racket to use depending upon his own style and standard of game. Only a few guidelines can be given here of what could be appropriate.

Elementary standard of play

To learn a stroke technique correctly one must be able to control the ball. A player could use a racket which produces great speed and spin and it may win him many points very quickly at a low level of play, but as he tries to progress to a higher standard of competition, he will not win points with the same strokes and he will need consistency in all his strokes. Consistency in a player's game needs to be developed first of all, so he should obtain a racket which according to the manufacturer's ratings gives a high level of control and only average speed and spin. To actually 'feel' the ball on the racket is very important at this stage of play because he will realise more clearly what spin and speed he is imparting upon the ball; therefore the' sponge and rubber should not be too thick. Although the service is a very important part of the game, there should not be too much emphasis on it in the beginner's stage because once again the beginner could win the point very quickly and so neglect practising stroke combinations involved in rallies. A racket that has a blade with good control and thin sandwich rubber will ensure that you do not obtain excessive spin on the service but at the same time the actual technique in serving will still be practised,

Intermediate standard of play

After acquiring the necessary control in the various strokes, a player or his coach should know what style he will try to develop: looping, counter attacking, defending, or a combination of any two or all three of these styles. There may still be a stroke where he does not have complete control so he may limit the thickness of the sandwich rubber on one side of the blade. He could therefore have a sandwich rubber which produces spin and speed on the forehand side and a thinner or slower sandwich rubber on the backhand side of the racket where his control is not so good. There are numerous possibilities regarding the combination of rubbers on a racket and they will depend upon a player's game, but the reader is advised to keep away from the really thick sandwich rubber rackets until reaching a high standard of play.

Advanced level of play

When a player has obtained a high level of control in all strokes and he has the correct footwork to enable him to move into position to play a stroke, he must consider whether he is obtaining the maximum speed and/ or spin on his strokes. Otherwise all the energy he is expending during the movement of the body could be limited in value. If he is consistently placing the ball in the opponent's court but the opponent appears to have sufficient time to move into position and then counteract the spin and speed on the ball then a blade or sandwich rubber that will increase the amount of spin and/or speed may be required. However, he should ensure that he can still accurately counter the opponent's spin and speed as well as impart spin and speed on the ball himself.

The price of table tennis equipment can vary considerably. At 1979 prices, blades can cost up to £ 11, and a sheet of sandwich rubber may cost 0. The price of some rackets is nearly £25. Why should a player spend all this money on, a piece of equipment when an article that costs only half the price may be more appropriate to a player's style or standard of play?

Racket blades can last a considerable time but sandwich rubber, through being a natural product, will become 'old' and will need replacing. An important point to know is when to change the sandwich rubber. Leading players in different countries frequently change their rubbers, especially if they play a game that relies on spin or speed of the ball from the racket. The defensive player who often depends on the control of the ball in his game may not change his sandwich rubber so often, as the rubber is increasing in control with age, but he must realise that the spin imparted on the ball by the rubber will be reduced. Certain manufacturers suggest that sandwich rubber should be replaced after sixty hours of play. At the highest level of play this assessment is quite suitable as the slightest loss of speed or spin in a sandwich rubber could be crucial to a player. However, younger or 'hard up' rubber so frequently, must try and compromise between the number of hours a sandwich rubber is used and the amount of money they have available for table tennis equipment.

Before starting to learn how to play table tennis, it is a good idea to familiarize yourself with the equipment needed and the terminology you will come across as you become more involved in the game.

There is a danger, when taking up a sport for the first time, of rushing out and spending a small fortune to kit yourself out, only to find out later that it was not the game for you after all. The end result is that a pile of expensive gear is consigned to the bottom of the wardrobe.

As far as table tennis is concerned, start off modestly. This is an accessible sport and by no means will you find it proves to be financially prohibitive. Look at the hundreds of thousands of Chinese youngsters who enjoy playing the game. The only piece of equipment they have to their name is the simplest of bats that you wouldn't even dream of using to dig the garden with in this country.

Investing in the best equipment does not automatically mean that you will become a great player. Equally, however, the Chinese approach is the other extreme and it is not suggested that you cut corners to that extent. Choose carefully, don't skimp but invest wisely in equipment which suits you and which will bring the best out of your game.

Buying a table-tennis bat these days can be a very confusing business, with manufacturers making all sorts of claims about their products. For the beginner—

and even the intermediate or 'club' player—here are a few simple guidelines to follow.

Handle These vary in shape and design but comfort is your number-one concern. If it looks flashy but feels terrible, then forget it, this is not the bat for you. The bat should feel natural and sit snugly in your hand without impeding your technique, allowing you to retain maximum control over all your shots.

Blade You do not have to buy a bat complete' these days. Most players have them made to their own specification by selecting, firstly, the type of wood and the number of plies to the blade and then choosing the appropriate rubbers to cover it. Until you become accomplished, your major requirement will be control and this needs to be reflected in the type of blade. Go for what is termed an 'all-round' blade of no more than five plies and made out of softwood if, at a later stage, you develop a fast attacking style, this would be an appropriate time to consider upgrading the blade to one of harder consistency.

Rubber This comes in two formats 'reverse' which is smooth with inverted pimples adjoining a layer of sponge, and pimples out which can be with or without a layer of sponge. Whatever rubbers you finally opt for, make sure they are embossed with the ITTF's stamp of approval otherwise you will be in breach of the Laws.

Unfortunately, this is not the only point to bear in mind when deciding upon a suitable choice of rubber. The most popular format is reverse and this can vary enormously in its speed and spin characteristics, Generally speaking, you will find that the harder and thicker the sponge layer, the faster the ball will rebound from the bat. The Laws state that the combined thickness of sponge and rubber should not exceed 4 mm. As a beginner, you would be well advised to sponge layer which is no more than 1.5 mm thick.

It is important that the overall combination you choose allows you to feel the ball on the bat. Resist being too ambitious at this stage, it's no good buying a super-expensive weapon if you cannot use it properly. In the long run, this will only prove to be a counter-productive short cut, because you will have become too reliant on the bat's properties and not enough on your own technique. The Japanese now have a National Under-11 squad made up of the country's most promising youngsters. None of them are allowed to play with anything but the thinnest of pimpled rubber. This is a material which gives maximum feel and control but has almost no spin or speed quality to it. Their aim is to groove in a flawless technique by forcing the youngsters to play the strokes and not become reliant upon the bat to do it for them. This should allow maximum benefit to be gained at a later stage when they pick up a bat with more sophisticated capabilities,

It is interesting to note that quite a few top players use a pimples out sponge rubber. Basically they fall into two categories, short pimples and long pimples. Generally the short pimples are used by attackers for hitting through their opponents' spin as they have a high degree of control but are not as good as reverse rubber for generating spin. The 1983 and 1985 World Champion Jiang Jialiang was a fine exponent of this

Champion Jiang Jialiang was a fine exponent of this technique. Long pimples are mainly used by what is now a comparatively rare species, the defender. They can be used to great effect against topspin by reversing the spin and returning the ball with very heavy back, Unfortunately, they do not have the same control as short pimples and players must weigh up the advantages and disadvantages of all the possible combinations before deciding what will, suit their style of play.

Table-tennis balls are graded in quality ranging from practice or 'one star' through to 'three star'. With a three-star ball you can be assured of a good consistent bounce with a longer life. A cracked ball will emit a chemical smell not unlike menthol. When this happens, get rid of it and replace it with a new one.

A full-size table measures 274 cm by 152 cm and stands 76 cm high. You can buy three-quarter size versions but you would be better starting the game on a full-size table. The playing surface should be around 2 cm thick and preferably no less. A thin table will give a poor bounce and affect your technique in the long run. Take care when storing the table after use. If it's a foldaway with its own undercarriage this should present little difficulty. It it's the loose-leaf variety, made up of two separate halves, make sure you store the two halves with their playing surfaces facing together. Try not to drag them along on their outside edges, this will only lead to chipping,

Looking the part and feeling right can be a real confidence-booster. A pair of jeans and your old training shoes might be OK for the occasional knockabout, but if you're serious about this game then decent-quality shorts, shirt and shoes are a must.

Shoes It is possible to buy shoes designed specifically for table tennis but they are not essential. As well as making sure that the shoes give good grip, pay attention to weight as well—they should be as light and flexible as possible. Support is also important, particularly around the heel and instep. You will probably find that tennis and squash shoes, while giving good adhesion to the floor surface, might be a little on the heavy side. If possible, try to find something a bit more lightweight.

Shirt/shorts Sports clothing is largely a matter of personal taste. Remember, though, that your outfit needs to be coloured in keeping with the rules which forbid white clothing. Clothing which restricts freedom of movement is to be avoided even though it may look impressive and fashionable.

Tracksuit A tracksuit is an excellent investment which will prove to be an indispensable asset. It is an ideal garment to wear when warming up and easy to slip on when the game is over, preventing muscles from becoming cold and stiff.

Holdall Your holdall should contain all those extra items which you are likely to need in an emergency, the most obvious example being a spare ball. Other essentials are:

1. a towel.
2. a couple of balls.
3. a spare shirt.
4. a drink.
5. some elastoplast.
6. a pen and notepad.

Table Tennis-terminology

Anti loop A type of rubber which was very popular amongst 'combination bat' players several years ago. It is very effective against spin as it gives virtually no adhesion to the ball.

Attack A style of play which is usually associated with players who drive and spin the ball at speed.

Backspin A form of spin which makes the ball rotate in an anticlockwise direction as it leaves the striking player.

Block A rebound shot which is played as soon as the ball bounces and requires little or no forward momentum on the part of the striker.

Carbon fibre A synthetic material used in thin film to form one or more of the plies within the bat blade. The Laws of the Game stipulate that at least 85% of the thickness of the blade should be of wood, so the scope for using it is fairly narrow. It has the effect of hardening the blade and overall making the bat a little faster.

Centre line The line running down the middle of the table and used to indicate the service areas during a doubles match,

Chop Another term for 'backspin', derived from the player's chopping action with the bat in order to impart a high degree of backspin.

Combination A bat with different rubbers on either side, each with different characteristics producing different effects on the behaviour of the ball, both in terms of its speed and spin.

Counterhit Sometimes known as 'flat hitting', this is a technique used against attacking shots and involves driving the ball hard without Imparting any spin on it.

Defensive A term often used to describe a style of play where the player is simply returning the ball, usually against an attacker but without necessarily forcing the play. 'Choppers' are sometimes incorrectly referred to as defenders. Although the style of ' play may appear quite passive, their clever and varied use of spin and deception often makes them the aggressor.

Drive A fast stroke which gives the ball speed and a small element of spin.

Dropshot A surprise shot which is played early in the bounce and close to the net when the opponent is some way from the table.

Flick A stroke produced largely from the wrist, often used as a way of returning various types of short service.

Float A shot with little or no spin on the ball; the way in which it is produced is designed to deceive the opponent into thinking the ball carries backspin.

Half volley A ball played very early in its bounce. Sometimes referred to as a 'block'.

Kill Also known as the 'smash', a shot which is designed to win the rally outright by hitting the ball as hard as possible.

Lob A defensive form of retrieval, used when forced away from the table. The ball is returned high into the air with topspin and deep into the opponent's half.

Loop A form of heavy topspin used to describe the way in which the ball dips in its flight.

Penhold grip A form of grip preferred by many Asian players where the neck of the bat is held between thumb and forefinger with the remaining fingers cupped or splayed across the back of the bat. The other side of the bat is used to strike the ball throughout play.

Push A short basic stroke, used to contain and control play, often during the early part of a rally.

Spin Spin occurs when the ball rotates on its axis during flight. It is produced when the bat's rubber surface temporarily grips the ball when contact is made. The direction of the rotation is governed by the direction in which the bat is brushed against the ball.

Third-ball attack This refers to the third ball of the rally immediately following the receipt of serve which often provides the server with an ideal opportunity to open an attack.

Topspin A form of spin which makes the ball rotate in a clockwise direction as it leaves the striking player.

Twiddle A technique favoured by many combination-bat players, It involves turning the bat in the hand during the rally so that both surfaces can, if desired, be used on both the forehand and backhand wings.

3

THE GAME

There are essentially four basic strokes in table tennis, which together form the cornerstone of today's modern game. They are:

- The 'backhand push' from which the backhand backspin or the defensive chop strokes stem.
- The 'forehand' drive which forms the basis of the forehand smash, block, fast drive and topspin shots.
- The 'backhand drive' which can also be developed into a topspin stroke or blocking stroke.
- The 'forehand push' which can also be easily varied to become a backspin or chopping stroke.

This chapter examines fundamental strokes and looks at the typical pitfalls encountered by beginners in the learning process. It also suggests one or two practices which can be coached to correct a fault, together with some useful exercises and games, designed both to groove in the shot and, at the same time, provide some enjoyment for those taking part. All the strokes are described as if they are being performed by a right-handed player. For left-handers, the same principles apply but read 'right' for 'left' and vice versa.

Backhand push

This is probably the easiest of all the four basic shots to learn. It's a gentle shot and is often used early on in a rally to keep the ball short and low to prevent the opponent from attacking. There is hardly any body movement involved and the stoke is produced at the elbow, with the bat held in a slightly open angle and travelling in a downwards direction to strike the back of the ball at the peak of the bounce. The feet and shoulders should all be square and facing the area of the table to where the ball is to be played. Whenever possible, the ball should be played just to the left of the stomach and not outside the body. This will make it easier to keep control over the direction of the ball. It follows then, that the player positions his body to where the ball is about to bounce, before the stroke is played. The correct stance, therefore, is all important.

Looking at the stroke in terms of the seven point checklist, it breaks down like this:

Length: Short

Timing: Peak

Table position: Close

Stance: Square

Body action: Nil

Free arm: Points to the ball

Bat arm and bat angle: Produced from the elbow, with the bat slightly open.

Fault correction

Problem: The player is hitting the ball too high.

Remedy: Check the bat angle to see whether by being

too open the bat is making contact withs the underneath of the ball and forcing it upwards. Check that the shot is being played using only the elbow, as many beginners tend to use the shoulder and lock the elbow joint. This can also have the effect of forcing the ball upwards.

Problem: The player has difficulty in playing the ball to a consistent length and overhits the end of the table.

Remedy: Check the grip. If the bat is being held too tight the arm will be stiff and it will be impossible for the player to develop touch and feel the ball making contact with the bat. Check the length of the stroke as well, as too much variation in swing will affect the distance the ball travels.

The main thing to remember about the backhand push is that it is a stroke used to control and contain play. Practices should be designed with this in mind with particular emphasis on consistency in both height and length. Whenever possible, try to avoid setting up practice routines where the shot is being played from the player's forehand side of the table as this is an unnatural occurrence in match play. With four right handed players on the table, however, it becomes unavoidable and in this situation vary the practice by playing 'down the line' as well as across the diagonal.

Exercises

For developing short 'touch' control the practice shown opposite is useful. It is especially valuable in helping those players who have difficulty in playing the ball to a consistent length. As a consistent stroke emerges, bring the players further back from the net in gradual stages.

Because there are not too many practise permutations possible with the backhand push, you might wish to try the following two fun games as a way of sustaining interest.

Game 1. This is a good way of occupying, four or more players on one table in an energetic way. Player 1 play, a backhand push along the diagonal shown to Player 2 who returns it also with a backhand push to Player 3 and so on, with all the players circulating around the table. Penalties can be introduced, for example, the first player to make a mistake has to perform five sit-ups or press-ups.

A useful spin off of this game is that it stimulates mobility.

Game 2. Using only the backhand push, both players must keep the ball within the area of two sheets of A4 paper joined together, which is chalked on the table. Play games of eleven up with points awarded when mistakes occur, including those occasions when the ball fails to hit the target area.

A target-related exercise such as this need not be restricted to the backhand push. It is designed to improve accuracy and also introduces a competitive element into a coaching session.

Forehand drive

Unlike the backhand stroke, virtually all forehand shots are generated from a side to square stance. In the case of a right-handed player, this means that the left foot should be leading the right slightly. The shot is produced from the shoulder with the elbow held at an angle of about 90° and the bat slightly closed. The bat moves forwards and in an upwards direction to strike the back of the ball at the peak of its bounce. At the same time, the weight should shift from the right to the left leg and the upper body should rotate so that the shoulders end up square to the line of play.

The follow-through finishes at a point roughly in line with the nose. Throughout the stroke, make sure that the free arm is running parallel with the playing arm and is being used to track the ball. It also plays an important part in helping the body to rotate in the manner described.

In terms of our seven point checklist, the forehand drive has the following characteristics:

Length: Medium

Timing: Peak

Table position: Close Stance: Side to square Body action: Rotating slightly Free arm: Points to the ball and helps balance and rotation of the body.

Bat arm and bat angle: Produced from the shoulder and parallel to the free arm with the bat slightly closed.

Fault correction

Problem: The player keeps overhitting

Remedy: Check that the bat angle is being kept sufficiently closed to ensure that the ball will be moving in a downward trajectory. Also, make sure that contact is being made on, or even slightly before, the peak of the bounce and not too late.

Problem: The player is unable to control the direction of the ball.

Remedy: Check the stance and body action. Are the feet side to square or is the body too sideways on? Are the shoulders finishing facing where the ball is to be played?

To encourage consistency, issue a challenge to the group and ask for the first table to produce ten, then 15, 20 and so on, good continuous strokes. The players on the losing tables have to perform five sit-ups, burpees or star jumps. If there's a wide disparity of ability in the group, handicap the more able pairs by imposing a higher target than the rest.

Backhand drive

This stroke is played with the feet in the same position as the backhand push, in line with the shoulders and facing the area of the table to where the ball is to be played. With the bat held at a slightly closed angle, the stroke starts just to the left of the body. Using the elbow, which should be held at about 90° or so, the bat moves forward in an upward direction, striking the back of the ball at the peak of the bounce, at a point which is just about left of centre of the stomach. At the point of contact, the wrist should be turning and folding the bat over the ball so that the stroke finishes with the forehand side of the blade visible to the player. The points to look for in a good backhand drive are:

Length: Medium Timing: Peak

Table position: Close Stance: Square

Body action: Nil

Free arm: Points to the ball

Bat arm and bat angle: Produced from the elbow and wrist with a closed bat.

Fault correction

Problem: The player is failing to turn the wrist and close the angle of the bat.

Remedy: Try placing a stationary ball on an open bat and tell the player to toss the ball like a sling shot over to the other side of the table. Without turning the wrist and folding the bat over thereby closing the angle of the bat, this will prove impossible.

Problem: The player is stretching for the ball when it is played wide or when it is played tight into the body, cramping the shot.

Remedy: The short answer to both of these difficulties is 'move your feet!' Make sure that the player positions himself to where the ball is played so that contact is made under the chin and in front of the stomach.

Apart from playing across the backhand diagonal, there is a limit to what you can do with this shot. Now is the time to combine this shot with the forehand drive.

Forehand push

Beginners tend to find this stroke the toughest of the lot. Its use and purpose in matchplay is the same as the backhand push and it requires a good deal of practise to master properly. The stance is the same as in the forehand drive slightly side to square but as with all strokes, the shoulders and upper body should finish the stroke square to the line of play. The shot is produced from the elbow and requires very little swing but it should not be a jerky action or the ball will fly off the bat. Held in an open angle, the bat moves forwards in a slightly downwards direction, hitting the back of the ball at the peak of the bounce and finishing just above the surface of the table. Although not quite as pronounced as the forehand drive, there should still be a little body rotation and the free arm, as always, can be used to pick out the ball and help with the balance.

To help control, encourage the player to get his head as close as possible to the ball without actually impeding the stroke. Using the checklist once more, the forehand push breaks down as follows:

Length: Short

Timing: Peak

Table position: Close

Stance: Slightly side to square

Body action: Rotating slightly

Free arm: Points to the ball and helps balance

Bat arm and bat angle: Produced from the elbow with slightly open blade.

Fault correction

The player has a tendency to alter the angle of the bat during the stroke and the shot starts to develop into a distorted version of the forehand drive.

Insist that the leading edge of the bat, that is the bottom part, lightly touches the table at the end of the follow-through. This will make sure that the bat is moving downwards and not across or upwards.

Instead of playing across the diagonal, set up the practice so that the stroke is played to a variety of positions on the table. Both players will have to take care that their stances are appropriately adjusted to maintain a continuous rally. Table tennis can be played as singles or doubles and as either men's, women's or mixed. Unlike other racket sports, such as badminton, tennis and squash, volleying is not allowed and the ball must be left to bounce on your own side of the table before you are allowed to hit it.

Most matches consist of the best of three games although in major international competitions this is often extended to the best of five, particularly in the main individual events. A game is won by the first player or pair to reach 21 points, or if the score is level at 20-all, the first to achieve a two-point differential.

Starting a game and serving

The toss of a coin confers on a player the right to make a number of choices. This can be to serve or receive first, whereupon the other player has the choice of ends. Alternatively, as the winner of the toss, you may choose an end, whereupon the loser may choose to serve or receive. Lastly, you can require the loser to make the first choice leaving you with whichever choice is not made by the loser. If you win the toss and choose to serve in the first game, you will be the receiver at the start of the second but the server once more at the start of the third.

After every five serves, the service passes over to the opposing player and this process continues until the game is over. However, if the score reaches 20-all, service is exchanged alternately until a winner emerges with two clear points. Unlike badminton and squash, points can be won or lost on the service.

There are a number of rules peculiar to the service which, if not properly observed, can be penalized by a point being awarded to the opposing player. These are as follows:

1. The service must bounce twice, once on the server's side of the net and then on the receiver's side.
2. The free hand, while in contact with the ball immediately prior to serving, must at all times be above the level of the table's surface for as long as the ball remains stationary on the palm of the server's free hand.
3. The ball must be thrown up from a stationary position on the palm of the free hand and not the fingers. It must be struck only on its descent.
4. When the ball is struck in service, it must be from behind the white baseline on the edge of the server's side of the table, or an imaginary extension of it should players choose to serve from a wide position.
5. The server has to ensure that the serving action is visible throughout to the umpire.
6. The service must not be farther back than the part of the server's body, other than his arm, head or leg which is farthest from the net. This rule sounds a little confusing but it is designed to prevent the server from turning his body away from the receiver and shielding the serving action from view.
7. If the ball brushes the net as it passes over to the other side, a 'let' is called and play stops. The server continues until a good serve is achieved.

Changing ends

Ends are changed at the completion of each game and if the match goes to a deciding game, ends are changed when one player or pair reaches 10.

The rally

The rally continues until one player makes a fault. There are a number of ways he can do this and the most common are:

1. missing the ball completely,
2. failing to hit it over the net.
3. missing the receiver's side of the table, perhaps by hitting the ball too far.

Other less common faults are dealt with in the 'Rules Clinic' chapter.

Scoring

This is fairly straightforward. There are two fundamental things for a scorer to remember. Firstly, the server's score is shouted first and secondly you must see that service changes hands after every five serves. An easy way to do this is to remember that this occurs when the two scores added together are divisible by five, e.g. 3-2, 14-11, 17-13 and so on.

Doubles

There are a number of rules which are unique to doubles but which do not feature in a singles contest. These are set out below:

1. You must serve from the right-hand side of the table and your service must land in the opposition's right-hand side. It is for this purpose that many tables feature a white line running down the centre.

2. You and your partner must hit the ball in sequence, alternately, until the rally is over. If you hit the ball out of order, your team will automatically lose the point.
3. After you have completed five serves, change places with your partner who becomes the receiver for the opposition's next five serves before commencing with his or her own set of five serves.
4. At the start of the second game, you must ensure that you are not serving to and receiving from the same player as you did in the first game, Similarly, if the match goes to a decider and you change ends at 10 points you must again swap places with your partner.

When playing table tennis, it is essential that one learns the most effective way of developing skill. The essential quality is to have insight into the required strokes and to be able to visualise all aspects of them, so forming a kinesthetic image. Then one must place the complete picture of the particular stroke into one's own game. Insight can be analysed as a process where a player may look at a stroke in a detached way and not just be obsessed by his goal. It is not good enough just to watch someone smash a really hard forehand and then be happy to be able to hit the ball as hard oneself, so that it goes on the table. One needs to appreciate the importance of each movement of the body beforehand, during the actual stroke and in the follow through, as well as the position of the body relative to the speed and direction of the ball. Apart from the player having the ability to analyse a skill, he must also make sure that the person whom he is copying is demonstrating the stroke correctly. If one has good insight, it will help development, and the knowledge gained can be transferred to one's own game. If one can learn to discipline oneself in normal working life, then it is likely that thoughts and behaviour on the table can be controlled. Many good table tennis players wishing to progress have learnt new methods which have failed to improve their performance because their insight into the learning of techniques is not adequate. To improve this insight, different theories of learning have to be studied and this is precisely what players and coaches should concentrate on.

Learning can occur through the formation of conditioned responses, but if the environment is slightly changed, a correct response does not occur. If a player learns to push a 'floated ball so that it returns every time to the other side of the table he has achieved this by learning, but if a heavy backspin push is then used by an opponent and the receiver uses the same push stroke, he will put the ball in the net. This means that learning involves more than conditioning, and psychologists have extended the use of the term 'conditioning' to include not only elementary reflexes but also any I complex of movements' which is in process at the time when the stimulus occurs.

One can learn a stroke by a method of trial and error, but this will always take far longer than being taught correctly. The more frequently a stimulus and response are associated with each other, the more likely it is that particular response will follow the stimulus. Therefore one has to practise in order to learn a skill. One cannot simply observe others and hope to perform the same skill without practice. So the well-known saying 'Practice makes perfect' is very evident if one wishes to acquire the kinesthetic image.

Making table tennis strokes with good technique involves very complex skills and in complex skills, wrong responses are more likely, at first, than correct ones. A player must acquire a type of feeling of movement and touch to accompany a stroke. The 'Law of Effect' states that 'A modifiable bond' (between stimulus and response) 'is strengthened or weakened as satisfaction or annoyance attends its exercise'. A player must remember not to get annoyed because more than likely this will detract from his concentration. Sheer repetition of strokes, unaccompanied by feeling, is not likely to have much result. Learning processes depend on rewards and satisfaction and correct knowledge of results. When learning strokes it is always a good idea to introduce the notion of a target so that if the player achieves his task effectively, he gets the feeling of reward or satisfaction. Players with poor techniques fail to find satisfaction because there is no sound basis for progress. So it is important that the player should get as near as possible to the correct stroke right from the beginning. Once a poor technique has been developed, further progress may entail a complete change and involve more difficulty than the original movement would have. This is because a bond has occurred between a stimulus and a response and this 'pathway' is difficult to alter. This means that if a player is used to stretching for a ball he then finds it difficult to learn how to get his feet into the correct position. If he cannot do this correctly the player could become dissatisfied and unhappy.

Before one learns a technique one must assess one's capabilities, such as maturity, strength and flexibility. It is no good for a really obese person playing a table tennis game to try to cover all angles of the table with his forehand loop drive because his physique will not allow it. He would be more likely to succeed at a crowding, blocking game over the table.

When practising, the player should be encouraged to respond to the stimulus in the way in which it is desired and the stimulus should never be presented when there are chances that some other response will occur. Therefore when practising a loop drive against a low backspin, a player should not loop a return that is mistakenly placed too high and which could be smashed, because he is being presented a ball to which he should react with A different response. If he starts looping this high ball in practice, the same is likely to happen in a match. Because a loop drive is usually a safer, stroke than a smash, many players have concentrated so much on looping that their forehand smash has considerably decreased in efficiency.

Players have to be able to adapt to external factors (visual cues). Examples are the speed of table, the type of floor and the size of the hall. They must learn to adjust to new conditions. English players who are so used to playing on fast tables are usually very good at counter attacking against each other, but when they go abroad and play on slower tables, their strokes do not propel the ball as fast. Thus the top European players have the time to react and produce a far more effective stroke, like a loop drive, and so be in a better position to dictate play. The way for English players to overcome this is to practise on slower tables, as they are now doing, Before a major championship., the ideal preparation is to practise in identical conditions. The English players now have the ability to play both the counterattacking game' and the 'looping game'.

One should not learn a set of strokes but should learn how to make strokes appropriate to the moment. This is the difference between a habit and a skill at the early stage of learning' Once these skills have been learnt they eventually become habitual. Environment varies little in shot putting, so a habit can be developed, but when the environment is constantly changing, as in table tennis, skill must be applied, When learning table tennis it cannot be overstressed that this is not Just a matter of acquiring a series of operations, one by one, and stringing them together. It is always the total organ Ism that does the learning and not Just those outer mechanisms that are most conspicuously invoked. When playing a stroke, it is not enough to hold the head and body in the right position and to swing the arm in the desired direction if these things are done without reference to each other. It is therefore vital that one develops correct 'motor intentions'.

Table tennis is a game where much attention must be given to the learning of strokes and to the interpretation of spin, speed and direction of the ball from the opponent. Motor skill psychologists define this as an open skill which has to fit either in an unpredictable series of environmental requirements, or in a very exacting series, whether predictable or unpredictable. In open skills like table tennis, a great variety of situations must be met and a player may counter stroke in such a way as to make up for his physical disabilities or bad techniques. Dragutin Surbek of Yugoslavia has been one of the best players in the world for many years, yet his backhand attacking strokes are seldom seen.

A table tennis coach must decide whether his players should have a good all round stroke ability or one or two dominating strokes. Stellan Bengtsson of Sweden is a player in the former category while Surbek is more in the latter mould.

Table tennis players need to build up strength, power and endurance to help prevent fatigue when, in competition, but one must not overlook the mental fatigue barrier which occurs, especially when playing someone of a higher calibre. Therefore one should realise that the central receptor, translatory and effector mechanisms concerning the organisation of data and the shaping of actions are working extensively in a game of table tennis.

When a player is playing someone below his own standard, there is the central receptor mechanism is a part of the body that receives different stimuli from the sensory organs of the body, The translatory mechanism tries to interpret the stimuli and less mental strain and this allows for longer periods of play without fatigue. Because he has more time to play his strokes, he is not using up the same amount of mental energy. The weaker player is using up much 'more mental energy because he is trying to think of ways of preventing the better player from dominating the game.

The weaker player is also likely to use more physical energy because the better player has more skill in placement and therefore is likely to make the weaker player move more. Mental fatigue can be eased in practice sessions by not initially making tasks difficult and so limiting the pressures on the central mechanisms. However, one should be careful that over concentration on the effector side does not lower the optimum level of performance.

4

LEARNING TO PLAY

Before actually discussing the various strokes and then the progressions to consistency and pressure play I feel it is very important to mention the various grips and ready stances which a player can use and how they can affect the strokes. There are basically two grips the shake hands grip used mainly in European countries and the penhold grip used mainly in Asia. Both grips have advantages and disadvantages.

Penhold grip

There are two main types of penhold grip the Chinese grip and the Japanese grip. In the Chinese grip the thumb and index finger are not as close together and the other three fingers are nearer the handle in such a position so that either one, two, or all three of them touch the racket. The advantage of the Chinese grip over the Japanese grip is that more movement is possible in the forearm through the pivot in the arm lever being the radio-ulnar joints and not the elbow joints. This allows for more power coming from a shorter stroke.

Definitions of strokes vary with the penhold grip. For example, if you talk to a penhold grip player about a backhand push, this is what he calls a block. Also his push is called a 'cut'.

The good point about the penhold grip style is that the position of the racket gives far more scope for flexibility in the wrist when playing forehand strokes or services. This is because the arm extensors and flexors are nearly always free for movement. The penhold players' grip also allows them to manipulate their fingers more easily up and down and around the handle of the racket and so delay the actual spin which they arc going to impart on the ball until the very]List moment. This timing makes it very difficult for opponents to react quickly for the return. The same reasons apply to the penholder being able to angle the short return of service on the forehand so well. With the shake hands grip wrist extension is limited and so the same range of movements does not exist.

Attacking strokes mainly consist of a type of block or smash. The backhand smash is played when a right-handed player has time to move his left leg back, which makes possible extra stroke preparation and more rotation of the hips and waist to impart more power. The block is played with a more 'squaret' stance and often the ball is hit more flatly than by the shake hands grip players. This is because the amount of topspin that can be imparted is minimal in comparison with the backhand loop drive or even topspin of the shake hands grip players. A flat ball can be very difficult for an opponent to return and the penholder's stroke can often cause great difficulty especially if he can angle the ball effectively. The movement from backhand to forehand in a penhold grip is much quicker and this is another reason why this is so effective over the table. Change of stroke can be done by movement of the wrist and radio-ulnar joint, whereas the shake hands grip players have to use the elbow joint more. This longer lever arm increases time in movement.

Shake hands grip

The big advantage which the shake hands grip players have is in their backhand stroke variation, i.e. push, block, counter attack, topspin loop drive, sidespin loop drive and smash. From the midfifties up to about 1970 the Asiatics had managed to dominate the Europeans even though Europeans had this advantage. However the Europeans had not developed their strokes to their full potential. Now that they have developed and can loop drive so well with the backhand they can avoid getting out of position so often by attempting a forehand loop drive. This also makes it more difficult for the penhold player to smash the ball. The penhold players do still try to smash the ball but the likelihood of error is greater.

Because of his more equal strength on both backhand and forehand the shake hands grip player also has the advantage when driven away from the table. He can retrieve quite adequately with both backhand and forehand whereas the penhold player finds it difficult to play a backhand stroke. Therefore the penhold player must try to get onto his forehand side and this requires more movement and the greater chance of getting out of position. A shake hands player therefore finds it easier to change his game from over the table to a deeper position if necessary, so as to give himself more time.

Ready stances

Before a player even receives a ball he may well be in danger of losing the point because he is poorly balanced or out of position, so it is very important to consider the ready stance. Certain principles should always be followed, The position of the feet should be marginally wider than the width of the shoulders. Balance should be on the toes so that a small piece of paper could slide Linder the heels. The knees should be inclined inwards through inversion of the feet and relaxed between flexion and extension to avoid imposing too much tension on the thighs. The stomach muscles should be held firm with the upper body inclined slightly forward and the shoulders be kept slightly in. The shoulders should be comfortable and not stiff or propped upwards. The arms should hang naturally because this is the angle of least fatigue and the elbow should be bent at approximately 90°. Adopt a position that is neither too close nor too far away from the table.

Attacking players who have strong forehand strokes often take up a ready stance. Attacking players who have strong backhand strokes prefer a stance nearer the centre of the table while defensive players take a stance in relation to the centre of the table and with the right foot more forward. These ready stances give each player the best opportunity of successfully receiving the serve and playing their stronger strokes.

Modern stroke play

Please note that the strokes are for righthanded players and they are described in set groups, i.e. forehand, backhand, attacking and defensive strokes. They are not necessarily to be taught in this order.

The forehand push

This stroke is used mainly as a safety stroke if a player

cannot play a more aggressive attacking stroke. It can be played from both the backhand and forehand court and can be very effective in manoeuvring an opponent. In its most effective form it is used when an opponent plays the ball short to your forehand with backspin. With careful manipulation you can play the ball back very short to any part of the table so the opponent cannot obtain a definite opening. A player who possesses good manipulation of the fingers and wrist can often angle the ball in the diagonal direction. If he feels that the opponent is too close to the table then the forehand push can be executed in such a way that the ball travels deep to the baseline. This shot must travel fast and have a good disguised spin on it or the opponent may be able to adjust his balance and perform an attacking stroke which may well be to your detriment. When learning this stroke it is best to play the ball to the middle of the opponent's right hand court and concentrate on playing the stroke with the correct footwork and the following principles.

When preparing for the stroke there is a transference of the player's body weight onto the right foot and the preliminary stance is such that the right foot is further back in relation to the 'square on' position of a 'ready stance'. One ensures that the body moves correctly so that the racket is moved behind the line of flight of the ball. As one has prepared for the stroke both legs should be flexed, with the left foot pointing generally in the direction in which you want to play the ball and the right foot pointing more towards the continuation of the base line of the table.

When coming in to meet the ball the racket will

start at approximately chest height with the elbow flexed at about 90° and the racket angle at just open. The more open the racket becomes then the more backspin will be imparted on the ball.

As the player's body weight is transferred from the right foot to the left foot the racket arm comes in a downward forward direction and contact will be made just in front of the body as the ball is dropping from the peak of its bounce. On contact with the ball there is a rotation in the forearm, and the ball will travel from the racket in an upward direction. The racket should almost be a continuation of the forearm; otherwise sidespin effects could occur on the ball.

This stroke is practised at first when there is little backspin on the ball from the opponent. A gentle guiding action by the use of left spinal rotation is a very important factor which must not be forgotten. It is important to remember not to follow-through too far, especially across the body.

The forehand counter attack

This stroke is used, against a counter attack or block when neither a smash nor loop drive is possible. The ball travels over the net so fast from the opponent that it is not always possible to find the time to move into a sideways stance, as for the push. One has to improvise by rotating the hips and thorax and pivoting sufficiently with the toes so that the ball is not struck with the racket while the body is too 'square' to the table.

The stroke should start with the weight of the player's body on the right foot. The player should continually watch the ball while rotating the upper body from the right. The elbow is flexed at an angle of approximately 90° and a comfortable distance from the side of the body. The shot is a relatively short movement and contact with the ball is made as it rises or reaches the peak of its bounce. Topspin is imparted to the ball as the racket comes behind and over the ball to about chest height. As one approaches the ball the player's body weight is centred mainly on the left foot. The angle of the racket on contact is slightly closed. On the follow-through it is essential that the racket does not travel too far across the centre of the body and that it does not finish above the head as this will mean that playing the next stroke will incur the return of the racket over the same distance, and often either this takes too long or one can become off balance.

The forehand flick

This is an attacking stroke usually used against a service or a push stroke played short over the net. The amount of speed that a player can impart upon the, ball will depend upon wrist-joint flexibility, timing and the height of the ball when it is contacted by the racket. Most attacking players rely on the forehand flick to create an 'opening' for them to follow up with a more forceful attacking stroke. The ability of the player to be deceptive in the placement of the ball is often more important than the speed of the ball, in enabling him to prevent the opponent from moving to play an aggressive attacking stroke. Ideally, a player should try to obtain a good combination of deception, angle of trajectory and speed when playing a forehand flick. When playing against a sidespin or sidespin topspin service placed to the forehand or the middle of the table, the right arm movements are very similar to a counter attacking stroke. However, when playing against a 'short' ball, the footwork is similar to that of a forehand push against a ball that has been pushed just over the net.

When receiving a push or backspin service, the racket angle will be closed and the precise angle will depend upon the amount of backspin on the ball. The contact point between the racket and the ball should be on the upper hemisphere of the ball and at the peak of the bounce. The racket moves mainly in a forward plane and slightly in an upward plane. If there is only a little backspin on the ball and it bounces 'short', but high, it may be possible to move the racket downwards towards the ball.

For the forehand flick to a short returned ball, a player should concentrate on positioning the right leg well under the table, which will necessitate a flexing of the right knee joint. The right foot should be pointing in the direction of where the ball will be approximately contacted. The left leg should not be over-extended or leave the ground, otherwise the body will be improperly balanced. If the left foot is positioned too far away from the right foot, the player will also find it difficult to move quickly into position for his next stroke.

When preparing to play the forehand flick, the player must anticipate the direction of the ball and where it is going to reach the peak of its bounce. He must then move his body so that his racket is positioned approximately one foot behind the expected peak of the bounce and in line with the flight of the ball. As the racket moves forward to make contact with the ball, the upper body should be inclined forward over the right leg and the right arm extended at approximately 165° at the elbow. The direction of the ball from the forehand flick can be altered at the last moment by varying the amount of flexion or extension in the wrist joint. The left arm is positioned away from the left side of the body so as to assist in balance during the stroke. The stroke should have a short follow-through so the player may move quickly away from the table for his next stroke.

The forehand smash

The forehand smash is usually played when a ball has been placed at a position on the table at a certain height so that you can attempt a shot which will not be returned by the opposition. It is normally very powerful and accuracy will only come with constant practice. Every player usually has a slight variation in the action of a forehand smash but certain principles must apply. It is necessary for a player to position himself so that he is going to make contact with the ball at the peak of its bounce or as it ascends or descends to shoulder height. If contact is made before these points there is a greater element of risk involved in the stroke.

To get in the preliminary position for a forehand smash, much will depend on where the peak of the bounce occurs. It is important that one gets the racket behind the ball in such a way that one is not off balance or stretching. For every forehand smash, one should position the body so that the angle of the racket is closed upon contact with the ball. This means that the main variable will be the movement of the feet over different distances to ensure the stroke remains similar, Sometimes A may only be necessary to pivot on the toe's of one foot while moving the other foot.

From the ready stance position one would move the right foot, then the left foot, almost simultaneously, so that the body is at a more side-on position to the table. The left arm is moved forward to balance the body as the right arm draws back to commence the stroke. The arm swing will vary according to where the height of the bounce will be, or if it is too high, then at shoulder height. The contact point will also affect the amount that the racket is closed'. When making contact with the ball it is essential that the body is moving forwards. The player's body weight should be on the toes of a flexed left leg during contact with the ball and as the follow-through occurs the degree of extension in the knee joint of the right leg should increase as flexion increases in: the knee joint of the left leg, but the right foot should try and remain in contact with the ground.

The player should watch the ball very carefully and the head and trunk of the body should move as one part. To ensure that the ball travels over the net correctly the follow-through should be in the direction of the ball. Only after completing the follow-through should one change the feet and body position in preparation for the next stroke.

The forehand topspin loop drive

This is one of the most useful strokes in table tennis but it is difficult to learn, There are many variations because it is a stroke which can be use against a ball that has been pushed, chopped, counter attacked, blocked or looped It should be a means of setting LIP the ball for a forehand smash i an outright winner cannot be achieved. Because so much topspin is placed on the ball it is very difficult for someone defending to keep the ball low over the net continually. More physical energy is used in performing this stroke than any other because there is a greater range of movement in all parts of the body and the speed of the racket on contact with the ball can be very fast.

As with the forehand smash it is important to try and get to a reasonable sideways stance and a wide base so that correct balance is kept throughout the stroke. The knees are flexed, more so than for any other forehand shot, so that the arm can draw the racket nearer the floor and the stroke will be longer and on contact with the ball the racket will have travelled further and gained more momentum. On commencing the stroke the player's body weight should be distributed mainly on the right foot and the right elbow should be extended to almost 180° while the left arm maintains body balance by being forward and flexed at the elbow.

As the racket travels up to meet the ball at the side or just in front of the body the racket arm becomes more flexed at the elbow, the knee joints extend, and the player's body weight is transferred onto the left foot while the toes of the right foot can remain in contact with the ground or the momentum of the rotation of the body can move it forward, Whether or not the rear foot is moving, there is d definite rotation of the hips and thorax so that the upper part of the body finishes in more of a square on position to the table. The angle and height of the bounce at which the racket contacts the ball will depend upon the amount of backspin or topspin imparted by the opponent.

If playing a topspin so that the ball is contacted as in 'A' the stroke is usually played at a time when the ball is descending. This stroke produces more of a lifting effect on the ball and is very useful against heavy backspin or push.

If playing a topspin so that the ball is contacted as in 'C' one has to have a high degree of coordination and skill. This contact point produces a fast speed plus spin and the contact point is at the peak of the bounce. The stroke can be effective against a light push, counter attack block or loop drive. The idea is for a vicious brushing effect to take place as the racket moves upwards and forwards. As with the other looping strokes the follow-through and racket deceleration should result in the racket coming above the head. From this position the whole body should return to the ready position for the next stroke.

At one stage in the history of the game it became quite easy for a blocker' to return a loop because nearly everyone had the same kind of spin oil the ball. So it was found necessary to develop a stroke which looked similar, but had a different spin variation, so that if the blocker attempted the normal stroke to counteract the topspin, loop, he would lose the point. Like the topspin loop, the topspin sidespin loop can be used against almost every shot produced by an opponent, but in the early stages of learning it is best used against a push or light backspin.

The position of the feet, left arm and racket are

very similar at the beginning of the stroke to the topspin loop but the actual racket movement will be different. The arm is kept straighter and, on contact with the ball, slightly in front of the body, the racket travels round its outside by a flexion of the wrist joint. The racket actually makes an arc shape from near the right knee out towards the right side of the table before coming in towards the centre of the body in the direction of the net. The body and right arm are moving as one during the rotational arc and the player's body weight is transferred onto the left foot. On the follow through, the racket could cross the face as a result of the momentum built up during the stroke. To achieve the correct stroke, the wrist is positioned so that the ball makes contact at the same point on the racket as the topsin loop but the top of the racket is facing more towards the ground inside of the side.

The forehand block

This has been a very important stroke especially since the introduction of the loop drive in the early 1960s. It is a good answer to the various types of spin imparted by the loop and it is now being proved that the once deadly loop drive is not so advantageous if someone masters its return. Depending on the amount of topspin and sidespin imparted by the loop, a player merely alters the angle of his racket on the block stroke to return the ball safely. Basically one judges where the ball will bounce, its direction after bouncing and the type of spin employed, and then it is a question of moving the feet to a position similar to that of the forehand push so that the racket is directly behind the ball, facing sideways and slightly upwards. An exception to this general rule is if the ball bounces short to the forehand. In this instance the right foot moves forwards to become the leading foot when contact is made with the ball. It' the ball is blocked with the forehand in front of the body then the racket will be pointing more upwards in a closed angle.

The stroke depends entirely on touch and it is essential that everything is done with perfect timing. The racket should be very lightly held and on the approach the whole body should be moving slightly upwards and forwards by means of a slight raising of the body by the toes. As contact is made with the ball when it is rising, there should be hardly any forceful movement of the racket and it should act like a cushion when the ball hits it. On contact, the arm raises the racket slightly forwards and so has a guiding effect on the ball, so that the topspin produced by the loop drive carries the ball back to the opponent. How well one can foresee how much spin is on the ball from a loop drive will determine one's success in countering it because the angle of the racket on the block will have to alter accordingly. This can only come with experience but if one remembers the cushioning effect then success should eventually occur. One must also remember that the heavier the topspin then the more the racket is 'closed'.

The forehand drop shot

In modern table tennis this stroke is not used very often because when two attacking players face each other, the opportunities of performing a drop shot rarely occur. The forehand drop shot is used when the opponent has been forced away from the table and is made to play a defensive backspin stroke to the opponent's forehand court. The ball will return just over the net and usually the attacking player can either smash the ball or play the drop shot. Most top players prefer to attempt the winning smash because they have all 'angles' of the table to aim at, but if they have been missing their forehand smashes they may find it safer to play the drop shot. If performed correctly, this should give the opponent little opportunity to return the ball, and if he does, it will be a scrambled effort so that he sets the ball up for the attacker to play a winning shot on the next stroke. It is more difficult for a player to perform a drop shot from a ball near to his own baseline as the ball may sit up so that the defender can move in and hit the return. The whole concept of the drop shot is to guide the ball just over the net into the opponent's court, so that if he left it, it would bounce at least twice before going off the table. It is therefore a sound theory that the nearer the ball is to the baseline then the more difficult it is to play the shot, because the distance the ball has to travel is further and the height of the parabola is greater, so as to allow for net clearance. The increased height and length-will tend to make the ball bounce more, and so there is a likelihood of it 'sitting up' or travelling off the end of the table so as to make it easier for the successful return.

When playing a forehand drop shot off the short return the following principles apply. The oncoming ball will be in a position to smash; otherwise the drop shot would be called a push. The ball therefore travels high over the net from the defender and bounces up high from the table. The attacker sees the opponent a long way from the table and in a good position to return a smash. The attacker perceives that he is going to smash the ball but at the last moment will change his stroke to the drop shot. In the preliminary stages one is in the final position to smash the ball with the racket comingdown to make contact and the player's body weight mainly on the front foot. As the ball reaches the top of its bounce one suddenly checks the stroke and rotates the forearm of the flexed right arm so that the hand travels from a pronated to supinated position. This involves the racket travelling, through an arc of about 85 and changing from a closed position to a very open one. Instead of coming down on the ball with a closed racket one will travel up to meet it with an open racket. During this time the player's body weight is being redistributed to both feet, though both legs are flexed at the knee joints, the left slightly more than the right. All that is required now, is for the attacker to move the racket slightly forward and up by a flexing movement of the shoulder joint. The impact should be very slight and only give enough momentum to the ball for it to drop over the net, The important things to remember are a 'loose grip' so one can obtain a cushioning effect on the ball and for the player's body weight to end upon the front left foot. There is little follow-through of the arm, or the ball will be made to travel too far and so ruin the effect of the stroke.

The backhand push

In top level table tennis this stroke is used less and less as the increased fitness of players enables them to get into position where they can play more attacking strokes like the backhand and forehand loop drives. However, it still serves as an important part of the game, especially if the ball is played really short with backspin on the backhand side, or if one's recovery from a previous stroke is a little too slow for an effective attacking stroke to be made. As in the forehand push, a flexible wrist and good arm mobility will greatly assist in placement that will not be detrimental to you. Once again you should try to angle the ball short or play the ball long if your opponent is cramped over the table.

The execution of the stroke is best learnt in the beginning stages by using a 'side stance' where the left foot is behind and to the outside of the right foot. If one wishes to dominate with forehand strokes the feet will be positioned in more of a 'square on' stance or with the right foot slightly behind the line of the left in relation to the edge of the table. It may not be possible to move the feet into the correct position in a quick rally so one must always improvise upon the two stances.

On preparing for the stroke the racket is brought back to the chest or slightly to the left of the chest and this movement is associated with the player transferring the body weight so that movement into the ball can use all the available guidance of the whole body. The elbow is once again at about 90° on commencement of the stroke and the racket angle is open. As the racket comes forward and downward to meet the ball, the elbow is extending, the shoulder is flexing and abducting, and the weight is being transferred to the front foot while the racket will come under the descending ball so that this time the forearm rotates towards a pronated position. The racket is again a continuation of the forearm and the follow-through should stop just before the forearm straightens or the racket travels too far across the body.

The backhand counter attack

This stroke is often used in table tennis and it is usual for an 'attacker' to have a very consistent backhand counter attack if he is to be a successful player. The objective behind the stroke is to keep the ball under control and then place the ball in a position so that one can follow-up with a winning stroke like a forehand loop drive or smash. In a game between two attacking players who do not have outstanding loop drives it is inevitable that many of each player's strokes will be the backhand counter attack, but it is interesting to note that against a defensive player it is very unlikely that the attacker will ever play this shot as it is not effective against backspin.

The player's body should be positioned behind the line of the oncoming ball so that if a stroke was not played the ball would make contact with the left side of the body. The left foot should be slightly in front of the right foot in relation to the line of the ball and the body should be balanced on the toes, while the knees are flexed in a jockey's position. The stomach muscle should be held firm, the chest pushed out and the eyes should be focused towards the white line at the opponent's end of the table. The left arm should be flexed at the elbow at approximately the same angle as the racket arm, as this will help in maintaining balance. The stroke starts from the waistline area of the body, with the hand kept below the line of the elbow. Contact with the ball should be made at the earliest opportunity above net height, preferably over the table. When contact is made with the ball, the racket face is slightly closed and it is coming forward and Upward to impart topspin. At this stage the arm will be in such a position that the hand and the elbow will be nearly parallel to the surface of the table. The follow-through should not be too long and should not come too far across the body, otherwise one may lose balance and fail to change position quickly enough for the next shot.

After considerable practice this stroke should be working like a piston and it is possible not to take the eyes off the far edge of the table because one should be able to develop an insight into where the ball is going to bounce. This does not apply if the ball travels to a position where another type of stroke will be necessary. The focusing of the eyes on the edge of the table instead of on the ball has two distinct advantages. Firstly, it allows one to keep a constant watch on the position of the opponent so one can be prepared to play a backhand quickly to a place beyond his reach. Secondly, this helps the player to see what type of stroke his opponent is likely to play and in what direction. If one jerks the head every time one plays a backhand counter attack this positioning sense becomes more difficult.

The backhand flick

If the mechanical principles of the previous strokes have been understood, there is little need to explain in depth the mechanics of the backhand flick, as they include certain principles of the other strokes.

When a push or service from the opponent is placed to the backhand court of the table, then the backhand flick can be used. It is used for the same reasons as the forehand flick and the racket is at a closed angle, the degree of which will depend upon the spin of the oncoming ball. The approach of the racket to the ball is similar to the backhand counter attack when returning a sidespin topsin service, and to a forehand flick when returning a backspin sidespin stroke, except that the right leg is placed forward, under the table, to assist in the balance of the body during the execution of the stroke.

The backhand smash

This stroke is best used when the ball is reasonably high in the backhand court and either there is not enough time or one is in too bad a position to move around and play the forehand smash. In modern table tennis when two attacking players play each other the ball is travelling too fast to play a backhand smash off a normal counter attack because there is insufficient time to place the feet and the racket in the correct position for the preparation of the stroke. Against the defensive player who is backspinning the ball. The backhand smash is usually a risky shot, especially as a forehand smash is dominant in the majority of players, and it is easier to teach the correct footwork to a player so he can move around to the backhand to play his forehand. Usually there is ample time to get into this forehand position because the ball is travelling a longer distance and at a slower speed than from an attacking opponent.

With the backhand smash it is important at first to get the body into a side-stance position. This is done by a small movement of the feet so that the right part of the hip slightly faces the table, with the right foot more forward than the left, and at such a distance that the ball can be struck at one of its highest points after the bounce. At the commencement of the stroke the weight of the player's body should be slightly on the toes of the back foot, but both feet should be firmly on the ground. The knees should be slightly flexed and the left foot should be nearly parallel with the end of the table; the right foot faces in the direction of the intended line of play.

The racket commences at about hip height and as it is brought forward to make contact with the ball, body weight is being transferred towards the front foot and as the thorax becomes more 'square' to the table the racket rises to just below chest height. The arm is beginning to straighten and the wrist is rotating so that the racket is coming over as well as forwards on the ball and imparting slight topspin. During the stroke the left arm is flexed at about 120"so as to assist balance. The ball should travel very fast and straight, so on the follow-through there should be more forward movement than upward movement. There should always be a closed angle of the racket on contact with the ball. After the follow-through the stroke should be decelerated quickly and then brought back to a ready position for the next stroke.

The backhand topspin loop drive

This is one of the most difficult strokes in table tennis. It is a very effective stroke for lifting heavy backspin services or strokes. A player who has not reached an advanced stage in table tennis would normally be happy to push the ball but this would be fatal because it gives the attacking initiative to the other player by enabling him to loop drive the long backspin return. There are numerous variations of backhand loop drives used on the Continent since many national coaches develop different styles of attacking players. There are general principles which are common to all strokes.

The ball is contacted just in front or to the left side of the body and although the positioning of the feet is almost the same as a ready stance, the knee flexion is greater at the commencement of the stroke. The left arm Assists in balance as in previous strokes, the chest and stomach muscles are held firm, but this time the racket starts from a lower position through the arm being more extended. As the legs extend at the knee joint there is a quick movement of the forearm so the racket is travelling very fast in an almost vertical plane. Just before contact is made with the ball, there is a quick wrist abduction action which further increases the speed of the racket. During con tact the racket moves slightly forward but the main emphasis is an upward movement so tremendous topspin is imparted and the ball travels across the net in an arc shape. The arc will become shallower if more forward emphasis is placed on the stroke.

The best contact point will depend upon the stroke used by the opponent, and it should be similar to the contact point chosen when performing a forehand topspin loop drive.

The backhand block

This shot can be used against the smash of an opponent but its accuracy involves an element of luck as the ball is travelling very fast when contact is made. One must hope that a reflex action will assist in placing the racket in the correct blocking position. As with the forehand block it is mainly used against an attacker who specialises in the loop drive.

The feet, body and arm positions are the same as at the start of the counter attack. As the ball is travelling towards a player he must judge the amount of topspin and sidespin upon it. He must then move the racket in line with the forearm and parallel to the near edge of the table. If the ball travels fast and high to the line of the body then it may be necessary to play a stroke vertically above the elbow so the racket is pointing towards the ceiling. As in the forehand block, touch and timing are vital. The racket is held lightly and on the approach to contact, the whole body should be moving slightly upwards and forwards by means of a gentle rising on the toes. The correct angle of' the racket, to cushion the ball will only come with experience but the general principle is that as contact is made the racket is brought slightly forward and upwards. The more topspin imparted then the more closed the racket face becomes. To counter sidespin, wrist movements are needed to make sure the racket face meets the direction of the ball at the correct angle. Little follow-through is necessary and so positioning for the next shot is quite easy.

The backhand drop shot

Few players use a backhand smash because they often find it easier to move around to the backhand court to play a forehand smash. Because a backhand smash is infrequently used it follows that a backhand drop shot should rarely be played. If an opponent is forced to play a backspin stroke and he plays the ball reasonably high and short to the backhand court of the table he can usually react more quickly to a possible drop shot because he can notice that the attacker is not moving around to play the forehand and he knows that there is generally a reluctance for players to attempt a backhand smash.

In the preliminary stages of the stroke the racket and body are in the backhand smash position. As the ball reaches the top of its bounce, the racket moving towards the ball alters its angle of approach as in the forehand drop shot. There is flexion in both knee-joints and on contact with the ball there is a gentle rising on the toes, a slight extending of the knee joints and the right arm moves forwards. A cushioning effect should result if one grips the racket loosely enough and the amount of forward and upward movement of the racket should just be sufficient to carry the ball over the net. There is little follow-through with the right arm, and the left arm, as in all other strokes, acts as an assistance to balance throughout.

The forehand backspin

As in the case of the simple pushing action on the backhand and forehand, the forehand backspin tends to be the more difficult stroke to master, especially the balancing of the body and the control of the follow-through during the stroke. It is usually used to counteract a loop drive or smash which has been placed in the right hand court of the table. The player should get behind the line of the ball and direct it in a line of flight which allows the maximum opportunity for the returning ball to hit the opponent's court, i.e. a diagonal direction. In more advanced play the defensive player should try to place the ball in the most awkward position for the attacking player to play a forceful stroke. The action of the stroke will vary according to the speed and spin already on the ball, but always the defensive player's aim should be to create the opportunity either to float the ball or backspin it heavily.

Let us first examine the action of a forehand defensive stroke which imparts quite an amount of backspin and then mention how one can disguise the amount of backspin. Against a topspin loop drive a player should judge the direction of the ball, and then move away and sideways to the end of the table so as to allow much of the speed and spin to be lost off the ball and preferably to make contact just above waist height as the ball is descending. The feet should be far enough apart to give a good balanced position. The left foot should be facing the direction in which the player wants the ball to travel while the right foot should be behind and to the right of the upper body with the toes pointing out to the side. The weight of the player's body should be on the back foot with flexion in the knee joint. The left foot should remain in contact with the ground and there should be a little flexion in the knee joint of the left leg, The racket should be held at about shoulder height with the arm flexed at the elbow, about six inches from the side of the body. Stretching should be avoided if possible, and all strokes should have a similar preliminary stage. The racket should not be held tightly and should be at an open angle of about 50°. The eyes are kept continually on the ball and as one approaches to make contact with the ball the player's body weight is transferred from the back foot towards the front foot so that the centre of gravity of the body is more central and both legs are more or less equally flexed at the knee joint. Body weight is on the big toe of the right rear foot and all toes of the left foot. As one comes to this position the racket is travelling towards the ball at an angle to counteract the spin. Contact should be made just above the waist at the side of the body with the elbow a few inches from the mid-abdomen area and flexed at approximately 90°.

The racket cuts under the ball to impart backspin, the longer contact can be made with the ball and the faster the racket can meet the ball, the greater will be the backspin produced. Extra speed of approach can be created by faster adduction of the wrist joint its one is just about to make contact with the ball. After the follow-through the racket will travel below waist height and body weight be transferred to the front left foot with the flexion in the knee-joint being more marked than in the rear leg which has almost fully extended. It is essential that the follow-through does not result in the racket cutting too far across the midline of the body. Throughout the stroke the left arm assists in balancing the body.

One must adjust the stroke to meet varying, amounts of topspin. If one wishes continually to impart a considerable amount of backspin on the ball one must make sure that if the opponent has put more topspin on the ball, then the angle of the racket should be less open and the descent to the ball more vertical, or more open and the descent to the ball more horizontal. If a player is really skilful lie can use a vertical backspin stroke to a ball which is still rising or has reached the top of its bounce. If one wishes to disguise the amount of backspin on the ball and actually not put much backspin on the ball, i.e. Float, the action is quite simple and can easily deceive the opponent. The speed of the racket is slowed up and on meeting the ball the racket moves more in a horizontal plane than a vertical plane or suddenly stops in its downward track.

The forehand topspin lob

This can be a very effective stroke but it is of vital importance that the stroke is administered correctly or the point is likely to be won by the opponent. It is used mainly against a smash or occasionally against a loop drive. A defensive player will usually try to backspin the ball but if he is out of position and stretching, he may find it more beneficial to play the topspin lob. An attacking player often prefers to lob the ball if caught in a defensive position because it sometimes offers more opportunity of getting into an attacking rhythm again and so avoids the possibility of getting permanently pinned down' to his weaker defensive strokes.

Some attacking players can be exceptionally good against the heavy backspin defensive players because of their excellent loop drives. It is quite noticeable, however, that many top players who have good loop drives have spent so much time Perfecting this stroke that they have tended to neglect practising the forehand smash. Consequently if a defensive player can perfect the topspin lob this really leaves his opponent no alternative but to try and smash the ball, which could well force him into errors. The ideal topspin lob should have plenty of height and topspin and land within six inches of the opponent's end of the table and so as to make him move to the backhand court to attempt a forehand smash. He cannot risk the difficult backhand smash, and he needs to wait for the spin to be reduced to eliminate the chance of error.

However, as he retreats from the table, the defensive player has the opportunity of getting into a good position for the next stroke. The alternative to smashing the lob is to block it, but this often gives advantage to the defensive player because he has limited the force and spin imparted by the attacking player.

The stroke is played when one is well away from the table and in the preliminary stages one can be in a more square stance to the table than the position for the forehand backspin. The left foot will be pointing towards the table while the right foot is behind and to the right side. The player's body weight is mainly on the toes of the right foot and both the knees are slightly flexed. The racket should be below waist height and the racket arm's elbow joint should be at about 140° and not too far from the body. The ball should be contacted as it is descending and the player's weight is evenly distributed to both feet and the racket is moving upwards.

As one extends the knee joints the racket is brought up at an open angle to make contact with the ball so that the correct topspin and height of trajectory are obtained. Usually this contact is at about chest height. The angle and direction of the racket on contact are vitally important. The angle of the racket and the speed of contact will affect the amount of spin on the ball, while the direction will affect the curvature of the parabola. The essential thing is to obtain a compromise so that with the racket sufficiently under the ball but coming up behind it to create lift, fineness of touch and control of speed will produce enough spin. On the completion of the stroke, the player's body weight should be on the front foot and the racket should be at about head height but not obscuring the vision.

The forehand topspin sidespin lob

This stroke has a similar effect to the topspin lob in terms of effectiveness against the attacking player The additional problem it presents to the opponent is that he has to core with a certain sideways movement as well as forward and upward movement of the ball off the table. It is used in the same instances as the topspin lob but it is performed slightly differently so as to provide the ball with a different path of flight. Really it is almost a defensive stroke becoming an attacking stroke because if administered correctly it can force the attacking player to play a safety shot and so lose the forcing initiative.

As with the topspin lob it should only be used when the ball comes on the forehand side of the table. If one attempts to play a forehand stroke on the backhand side, the whole of the forehand court is 'left open' and this area will often be monopolised by the opponent with the next stroke. If any lob drops short of the baseline by more than a foot then a reasonable attacking player can make the defensive player pay dearly for his mistake.

The footwork in the preliminary stages is the same as in the topspin lob but there is a difference in the arm action which causes a different angle of approach to the ball. The racket is held below waist height, while the body weight is on the back foot as in the topspin lob. As the body is moved towards a more forward position the balance is distributed equally on both 'feet. The racket moves upwards as if to make contact underneath the ball Nit then the wrist is flexed so that the racket can contact the outside of the ball. The contact point occurs with an open racket between waist and chest height at about one foot from the body, as the ball is descending, but by the time the ball leaves the racket the racket should be further up and away from the body. A rotation to the left by the thorax will assist in the arc movement of the right arm, which will affect the amount of spin that is put on the ball and also influence the follow-through. The player's racket should not pass too far across the centre of the body and the weight of his body should be on the left foot at the end of the stroke. By the completion of the stroke (including the follow-through) the position of the player's body should be square to the direction of the ball.

The backhand backspin

This is nearly always the defensive player's most used stroke against his attacking opponent. The reason for this is that most players are right handed and the most ineffective stroke of an attacker against the defender is the backhand topspin. Most defensive players therefore play down the backhand side of their opponent and this necessitates the frequent use of the backhand backspin. Once the attacking player moves around to play the more effective forehand strokes, the defensive player can then start changing the direction of his backhand backspin to force the attacker into errors connected with moving and positioning for a stroke. The position of the body and angle of the racket on contact with the ball can be influenced by the speed and spin imparted by the opponent. The action of the strokes against a loop drive that is not too excessive can be as follows:

As the ball is approaching one should judge the direction and make sure that the feet are positioned so that the racket is behind the line of flight. In the preliminary stages the weight of the player's body should be on the back foot, which should point in a line reasonably parallel to the end of the table, while the right foot should point towards the table. The left knee should be flexed while the right leg is reasonably straight. The eyes should be kept on the ball and the racket arm flexed so that the racket is positioned near the left of the left shoulder. When approaching the ball the player's body weight becomes evenly distributed on both feet and the racket comes down in an angle of declination so that it will cut under the ball. During the contact with the ball the player's body weight is transferred to the front foot so that the right leg becomes more flexed at the knee joint and the left leg extends. The racket meets the ball at an open angle of about 40° to the horizontal and if extra spin is necessary one can use a quick abduction action of the wrist to create extra speed of movement of the racket. As explained during the forehand backspin, extra spin can be obtained by moving down or under the ball at a greater angle or by increasing the speed of approach.

When applying heavy backspin by coming down viciously on the ball the stroke will 'necessitate the follow-through of the racket to below the waist but not as far in front of it as with the previously described stroke. This is a more difficult stroke to perfect. However, it is very important to learn because it may be required against a severe loop drive if one wishes to play the ball near the peak of the bounce. During all these strokes it is essential to try and have a sideways stance and never to bring the racket too far across the body, otherwise balance will be severely affected. There is, however, an exception; it is usually in the 'float ball' stroke that it occurs.

When a ball is looped or smashed to the body it is usually easier to get into a satisfactory position with the backhand defence than with the forehand defence. One often does not have time to move the feet into the correct position for the backhand stroke and so one is committed to have the whole body behind the line of flight of the ball. In this case one must abandon the preliminary stage, when the racket should be about six inches outside the left shoulder, at shoulder height. When one is caught in this square position' it is best to have the same degree of flexion in both knee joints and have the heels just off the ground. The racket should start its descent just below chin height and travel with an open angle of about 20 to the vertical line to meet the ball. The final angle will depend upon how much topspin one has judged to be on the ball. During the follow-through the racket will suddenly stop its downward projection and move in a horizontal direction towards the table by an extension of the elbow joint.

The 'floated ball' has little spin and if the stroke is administered correctly it can create difficulties for the attacker because he will have to play a completely different stroke in order to ensure that his next stroke does not send the ball off the end of the table. The float backspin can be used in any position but when the ball is not straight at the body one can position the feet correctly as in the backhand heavy backspin and the preliminary stages will be similar, although the contact and follow-through are different and prescribed as above.

The backhand topspin lob

Like the forehand topspin lob this can be a very effective stroke but it must have the correct height and length in the parabola it describes in order to make it bounce near the opponent's end of the table; otherwise it will most probably be smashed by the opponent. It is used in similar circumstances to the forehand topspin lob both by attacking and defensive players, except that the ball is on the backhand side of the table. When the ball I's coming fast towards the body and one cannot move into the correct position, the backhand lob is preferred to the forehand lob. The position of the feet is similar to the backhand backspin.

One should not be overstretching for the shot or be off balance, and at the commencement of the stroke the knees should be flexed and the racket positioned below waist height on the left side of the body. On contact at the side and in front of the body, the legs should begin to straighten and the racket should come up and over the ball after the initial stage where it is behind and below the ball. The speed and fineness of touch will determine the amount of topspin that will be imparted to the ball. On completion of the stroke one should remain balanced with the racket extended in the air at about head height but one should avoid losing sight of the ball.

The backhand topspin sidespin lob

Like the topspin lob this can be a very important stroke if performed correctly and it can convert a defensive game into an attacking game if used at an opportune time. However, it is unlikely to be used by a purely defensive player unless he is in a desperate situation and cannot play a sound backspin stroke or because the attacker can play better against backspin than sidespin. It is used under the same circumstances as the forehand topspin sidespin lob except that the ball will be on the backhand side of the table. It is also one of the most difficult strokes to play for a defensive player or for an attacker forced into a defensive position and only a few players in England really use it effectively. As with most lobbing strokes, one must have very good footwork to move into the correct position, otherwise the ball will not gain the necessary spin, speed and length to prevent the opponent making a winning smash.

In the preliminary stages of the stroke the feet should be in a position similar to the topspin lob but the racket should he positioned approximately below waist height and nearer the centre of the body so that one has plenty of opportunity to create a sidespin as Well as topspin movement. On contact with the ball one should rise on the toes and through the shoulder and the elbow joint the right arm should bring the racket forward and upwards to meet the ball with an open face at about one foot from the body. This time the racket comes from behind and below the ball, then makes contact around the left side so as to impart topspin and sidespin. Once again there has been a wrist action producing movement from a pronated to a more supinated position. On completion of the stroke the weight of the body should be more on the front foot and the racket should not obscure the player's vision.

Stroke combinations

It is essential that a player learns the correct techniques involved in producing a stroke at the earliest opportunity. Once he has an understanding of the correct grip and stance required for his particular style of play, he should ensure that with each stroke he is moving his body in the most economical fashion to produce the required amount of spin, speed and direction on the ball. Movement of the feet should not be excessive at this level until the player has a complete understanding or what each part of his body is supposed to be doing during the preparation and follow-through of each stroke. Although the direction of the racket during the build up, contact with the ball, and the follow-through of the stroke is essential, the player must also realise that the movement of the arm alone is not sufficient to produce power in the stroke or consistency and accuracy in the placement of the ball. The best way of learning a stroke is to have practices which involve one player using a stroke against another player who consistently returns the ball with a stroke that is likely to be played in a game. At the beginners stage they are each learning one stroke instead of combining two or more of their own strokes in the same rally. The movement that will be necessary will be minimal in comparison with 'pressure play' practices and this will provide a better opportunity to learn the basic principles involved in the stroke. A player may become bored during the learning of the correct technique of a stroke so he or his coach should try to set challenge; regarding the number of successful strokes and the accuracy in placing the ball.

To commence with, players should concentrate on learning the push, backspin and topspin services, return of service, counter attacking strokes and the forehand smash. When they have become reasonably efficient with these strokes, simple stroke combinations can commence but footwork should be limited. An example of this is with pushing strokes where both players use forehand and backhand strokes alternately but the players try to direct the ball to a place on the table where the opponent needs to move a minimal distance. When these combinations of strokes have become reasonably efficient, players should progress to learning the forehand loop drive (at the beginners stage a stroke which imparts topspin will suffice), the block and the backspin defence. Stroke combinations are similarly introduced, then the length of the return is varied, then the direction.

To make stroke production a little easier in the beginners stage the player should play each particular stroke at the same contact point in relation to the height of the bounce of the ball and he should concentrate on varying the follow-through of the stroke to alter the length of the return. The speed and spin on the ball should be negligible at the beginning and only be built up as consistency improves.

For each stroke it is best to return the ball in a diagonal direction, then down the side line of the table, then in a straight line from the middle and finally in a diagonal line to the corners, from the centre of the table. Do not try to play a forehand stroke down the diagonal or middle from the backhand court until all the other exercises have been attempted.

The direction of the feet and shoulders in relation to the table will depend on whether one is playing down the diagonal or side lines of the table and from where on the table one is playing the stroke. The general rules for forehand strokes are to have the feet positioned so that the lateral view of the shoulder of the non-racket arm is facing in the direction of where the ball is intended to travel, so that the racket is moving towards the ball in the line in which the ball will be played. The body should be well balanced and the elbow of the racket arm should not be cramped into the side of the body. The rear foot should be the right foot with the right-handed player and it should be angled at about 90° to the intended flight-path of the ball.

The position of the shoulders when playing a forehand stroke from the middle of the table. It is the same for a penhold or shake hands grip player. A forehand stroke down the diagonal line or the table from the backhand court while a forehand down the sideline of the table from the backhand court.

With the backhand counter attack and block the footwork variation involved in playing to different parts of the table is much less. The important point to remember is that the player should align his feet and shoulders in the direction in which he intends to play the ball. It is difficult to serve short with topspin services, Therefore this skill should be left, as with the sidespin service, until the intermediate stage.

Short backspin services should be pushed and topspin services should be counter attacked and chopped in the beginners stage. With these practices, the receiver can start to learn counter attack and backspin strokes.

Counter attacking strokes

In practising this stroke it is helpful if the opponent returns the ball high after he has made a number of counter attacking or defensive strokes. A player should be capable of forehand smashing the ball to anywhere on the table, from any position, when it is at a sufficient height.

The player should now have the ability to develop his skills in table tennis by learning the more difficult strokes and services. The sidepsin topspin and sidespin backspin services, backhand loop, backhand smash, forehand sidespin loop and topspin lob strokes can all be learnt with similar practices to the strokes used in the beginners stage. He must learn the technique of imparting sidespin on the ball and also learn to combine different strokes over a wider range of movement. The degree of movement will be more excessive than in the beginners stage; therefore the footwork practices are essential so that the player is in the correct position to play a stroke. In a game situation the player only has a few hundredths of a second to decide on the direction and spin of the oncoming ball and then move into the correct position. To position himself correctly a player will have to be able to move diagonally, backward or forward. It may also be impossible to meet the ball at the same contact point for a particular stroke, so it is necessary for a player to practices playing strokes before the ball reaches the top of its bounce, also as it reaches the top of its bounce and as it descends after it has reached the top of its bounce. A player must also learn to vary the speed on the ball so he must practise soft, medium and hard strokes. Players should always commence by playing slow, controlled strokes.

The following training exercises could be used in the intermediate stage: Key—1, 2, 3, 4 etc.—The position of the placement of the ball on the table.

Backhand practices for consistency

These are being performed as the opponent is practising his side to side movement skills.

Practices for speed

Practices for speed of the stroke can be similar to those of consistency play. A player should set a target to achieve with each stroke and then see if he can play the chosen number of repetitions at a slow speed, a medium speed and finally at a fast speed. When he has become proficient with these sequences he should then try to play a smaller number of slow, medium and fast strokes but keep repeating the sequence in the same rally.

Practices for the length of the stroke

Once again the same sequences can be used but this time targets are placed on the table at different distances from the net.

Practices for different timings of the ball

As in the practices for the speed of the stroke the player decides on a number of balls he will play at a certain timing point and eventually he will play different timing points in the same rally. Examples of what is meant by early timing, peak timing and late timing:

Practices for strokes played at different distances from the table

These sequences involve movements over far greater distances and in many different directions. Both players should concentrate on performing these exercises with a slow, consistent stroke that is accurate in direction and imparts little spin or speed onto the ball. The variation of direction, speed, spin and length of stroke should be left to the advanced stage. There are numerous exercises which players can practise to suit their own style of play. Once the following exercises are being achieved with a good degree of success over a wide range of strokes a player should be approaching a high level of performance. The footwork practices in moving from one position to another are very complex and many top players learn different techniques even though their styles may be similar. Certain players make up for their poor footwork by good reflexes and hand-eye coordination. All the top players can be caught out of position during 4 game and they have to use improvised strokes to counter their lack of balance but all of them try to obtain a balanced position to play a stroke if it is at all possible.

During the beginners and intermediate stages all the exercises were very predictable. This meant that the player knew where the return of the ball was going and he was moving in the required direction before the ball left the opponent's racket. The rhythm of the movements was also predictable,, as the player rarely had to move rapidly in a continuing zig-zag formation. Further, all the exercises had stressed consistency in a high number of repetitive movements. In the advanced stage, exercises must be practised so that the player does not always know where the ball will be travelling and he must be able to play strokes that vary in direction, length, timing, speed and spin.

A player should now be concentrating on practising sequences where he tries to win the point from the service, return of service, third, fourth and fifth stroke, because in many matches over 75 per cent of points are won before the sixth stroke of the rally. A high level of physical fitness is a very important requirement for performing exercises well in the advanced stage. Pressure play exercises on the table as well as physical conditioning in the gymnasium can be used to develop stamina and mobility in the individual. There are many permutations of exercises that could be practised but it is at this stage in a player's development that he must make a critical self-assessment of his own game. He should then create exercises that will both improve his strengths and eradicate weaknesses.

Desmond is a left-handed attacking player who has very good backhand strokes. He has good reflexes and flexibillity and he has a remarkable hand-eye coordination that allows him to have a very good timing with the ball. He is also very agile and he moves very quickly when in a position close to the table. He lacks the ability to impart vicious spin on his services but his return of service is very good. He is comparatively weak when caught in a position away from the table or when stretched wide to the forehand. He also lacks power in smashing against the high topspin lob defence and he does not like playing against consistent flighted topspin. Like all the other English players it was necessary to try and rectify his weaknesses so that he could create a position to dominate with his strongest strokes.

Practices: Service practice. Receive of service practice. Service and follow-up practice, known as a third ball attack. Receive of service and follow-up practice, known as a fourth ball attack. Service, placement and follow-up. Known as a fifth ball attack. General weakness practice.

Before a serious back injury in 1976, from which he has only just recovered, Nicky was one of the finest players in the world against defensive player's. He is an attacking player who has a very good loop drive and a wide variety of accurate services. His main weaknesses are his backhand attack and his receive of the service short and wide to the forehand.

Practices: Service practice. Receive of service practice. Third ball attack. Fourth ball attack. Fifth ball attack. General weakness practice.

Paul is a left-handed attacking player with a very good variation of forehand services and forehand loop drives. He has a good physique and he is very quick in his movements around the table. He uses his fitness and mobility to try and move into positions so that he can dominate the game with his forehand strokes. His backhand attacking strokes are weak and he is vulnerable when receiving short services and when playing against good defensive players.

Jill won the Ladies Singles and the Ladies Doubles, partnered by Linda Howard, in the European Championships in Prague in 1976. She is one of the best defensive players in the world but she can also attack very well with her backhand against the push ball. She has a weakness against players who can notice her variation of defensive strokes and who keep looping the ball with high heavy topspin. She is also weak if she tries to attack with her forehand against defensive players who place every ball down her forehand.

Practices: Service practice. Receive of service practice. Third ball attack. Fourth ball attack. Fifth ball attack. General weakness practice.

Carol is an attacking player who has one of the finest forehand loop drives in women's table tennis. She has a good variation of services and her backhand loop drive is improving rapidly. Once she has improved her level of physical fitness she is capable of reaching a standard comparable with the best women players in the world. Carol is weak against players who can involve her in long counter attacking rallies or players who can loop continuously against her.

Practices: Service practice. Receive of service practice. Third ball attack, Fourth ball attack. Fifth ball attack. General weakness practice.

There are numerous exercises that can be practised which will develop stamina, power and mobility in the individual. These exercises involve rapid movement over a short time in a conditioned or unconditioned direction. The following examples could be practised. The player must play forehand counter attacking strokes from position one, then position two, then he must move and touch the net post on the right side of the table with his racket he must then return to position one and continue the sequence until an error is made. The opponent should stand about two yards away from the table and play slow backhand counter attacking strokes alternatively to positions one and two. As the opponent improves, 'the feeder' can stand closer to the table or increase the speed of his stroke so that the player who is using the forehand strokes has less time in which to move.

The practice is similar except that the player touches the net post on the left side of the table with his left hand, and the feeder uses a forehand counter attacking stroke.

The player pushes the ball then moves back to touch a marker on the floor approximately ten feet from the edge of the table; he must then return to push the next return and the sequence continues until a mistake occurs. The feeder pushes the ball slow and high at the beginning and he increases the speed of the return as the player improves in his movements about the table. The player can push the ball with the backhand or forehand and he can touch the marker with his racket or his left hand. The actual stroke and touching of the marker will depend upon the position of the ball on the table from the feeder. This exercise is very useful for defensive players, and the top players can place the marker more than ten feet from the end of the table.

Three markers are placed on the floor and numbered one, two and three. As the feeder serves or pushes the ball, he calls out one of the marker numbers. The player must then push the ball and move to touch that marker with either his racket or left hand and then return to a position so that he can push the next stroke and move to the next or same position, that the feeder may call.

A good practice for players is that of placing the ball towards the right hip of the opponent. Many players have difficulty in moving their feet so that the body is to the side of the oncoming ball when they play a forehand stroke. They must move to allow their right arm to make the correct approach towards the ball. Therefore after a player has looped the ball the opponent should try and work out where the player's recovery stance will be and then block the ball towards his right hip. This practice is excellent for developing precision in the stroke of the feeder and feet movements of the looping player.

Service and the return of the service

Many people consider the service as a stroke which starts off the rally and only introduces the ball into play. This theory of the service was evident in the decades when pimpled rubber rackets were mainly used but with the introduction of new rubber and sponge, tremendous spin can be imparted upon the ball and the service is now more of a pointwinning stroke. In recent years the service has been developed enormously, especially by the Asian players. Even when internationals are playing against each other it is not uncommon to see a player with a very good service winning as many as seven points in a game through his services not being returned. It is quite probable that the receiver could return the ball onto the opposite side of the table, but it is important for him to place the ball so that the server cannot create a winning follow-up stroke. It is mainly because of the receiver's attempted meticulous placement that errors occur. If the receiver's positioning, timing or interpretation of the spin is slightly wrong then the server has produced a stroke which usually results in the return being placed high or into the net. If the ball is returned high the server usually plays an attacking stroke and often wins the point.

So far we have noticed two aims of serving in modern table tennis. The main aim is to win the point and the secondary aim, if the main aim fails, is to position the ball so that a good follow-up stroke can be played. The type of serve used will often depend on the style of the opponent. However, no matter what service is used a player should serve so that the receiver's return cannot cause excess movement for the server during the follow-up and result in an unbalanced body position. Really the service is like the opening moves in a game of chess in that it lays a foundation for the rest of the point. Depending on the opposition, a player will generally use a service which is directed to a point on the table where the opponent is forced to use his weakest stroke and therefore prevent him from gaining too much initiative during the rally. At the same time the server will try to use a service with a type of spin imparted on the ball so that the return has a good chance of being directed to a certain portion of the table. The server will have practised this serve for many hours and also the variation of follow-up strokes depending on where the return is made.

There are defensive and offensive players, left-handed and right-handed players, forehand dominating and backhand dominating players, so it is very necessary that an accomplished player can perform services with all types of spin and speed to different parts of the table so that he can play on the weaknesses of all opponents. A simple example of the importance of a variation of service can be indicated by a right-handed player who prefers to play a counter attacking game and he often becomes involved in this type of rally by serving fast down the right-handed opponent's backhand so that he is likely to play a backhand counter attacking stroke. If the server was playing a left-handed opponent and he tried the same service he would be serving to the opponent's forehand and this might result in that player doing a loop drive and so causing the server to 'block' rather than play the counter attacking game that he prefers. Therefore, it is very important that the server can make a good fast service down the line as well as across the diagonal so that he can play on the left-handed player's backhand.

Deceiving the opponent

Services are made with either the backhand or forehand side of the racket and they consist of either topspin, backspin, sidespin or a combination of topspin and sidespin or backspin and sidespin. The spin imparted on the hall will depend upon the preparation, contact Lind follow-through of the racket with the ball.

The most important aspect of serving is being able to deceive the opponent without breaking any of the laws on serving. Obviously, a player needs to practise services so as to obtain the length, direction, speed and spin which he requires, but all the time he should be concentrating on having almost the same preparation for a particular service as he would have for another service which may be completely different in either spin, speed, direction or length. It is the ability to change the direction of the racket when about to make contact with the ball that often produces a good service. The nearer to contact with the ball that the racket direction can be changed, the less time the opponent has to interpret the spin, speed, direction and length of the ball.

The way in which a player grips the racket when serving can alter the amount of spin imparted on the ball, the speed of the racket and the speed in the change of direction of the racket. The penhold grip allows more flexibility in the wrist joint when serving and consequently greater ranges of movement with quicker changes in direction. Shake hands grip players try to increase their range of movements in the wrist joint when serving by placing the hand further down the racket handle or by loosening or changing the position of their fingers around the handle. The ball can be contacted in many places by many parts of the racket to produce a similar type of spin. The more skilled a player becomes in his ability to make a similar serve by using different parts of the racket and hitting different parts of tile ball then the more useful his services will become.

A player should have the ability to throw the ball up at different heights and still make the same service. The variation in the trajectory of the ball will keep the opponent guessing and possibly create an error in balance or movement.

Before releasing the ball from the hand, look carefully at the opponent's position in relation to the table. It could well be that he has taken a different ready stance because he has seen the server preparing to make a certain service and this new stance could result in the receiver gaining the initiative from the service. The server must then decide whether it is worth attempting that particular service or trying to serve to another part of the table so that the receiver has a greater distance to cover, even though it may be to a stronger department of his game.

An opponent can occasionally take up a ready stance slightly closer to the table or slightly farther away than intended, so in the viewing of the opponent the server should decide what service would be most effective through the opponent's error in the preparation for the receive of service. If he takes up a stance too close to the table then a long deep service could be effective or if he is positioned too far away from" the table a short service down the forehand may be appropriate. The actual distance of a player from the table edge in the ready stance position will depend upon his size and style of play and the above figures are only examples. A good method to commence with is to stand one arm's length from the edge of the table.

It may be necessary to change the service completely from a backhand to a forehand stroke. A new serving position in relation to the table could therefore be created and the amount of time taken to change positions could irritate the opponent and he may not take up the ideal receive of service position.

General body movements when serving

The precise body movements will depend on the particular service being performed but there are generally three categories of body movements. Some players are very flexible in the wrist joint and they can obtain a great amount of spin on the ball through a short quick wrist action. Other players use the whole of the body when serving and they build up the 'forces' through the body joints so that when contact is made with the ball the racket is travelling very fast. Some players contract different muscle groups in their body in such a manner that on movement towards the ball extra momentum is gained by a coil effect which is transferred to the racket arm.

No matter what method is used when one is learning to serve, one should aim to serve the ball so that the body and toes of the leading foot are pointing in a direction common to the path of the ball. Once the ball has left the racket then one should consider the next position to move into so as to counteract the return. After one has mastered the quality of touch and body coordination, the really talented player can start another method of deceiving the opponent, by serving in a direction completely alien to the direction of his body. Contact between the racket and the ball should not be made too far away from the longitudinal axis of the body, otherwise it is possible that the body will be in an unbalanced position and precision in placement of the ball will be more difficult.

Another general principle that is very important is not to have the feet too wide apart on completion of the follow-through stage of the service as this will make the recovery to the next position slower. The player should also be very careful about the length of the stroke after the ball has left the racket because lie must allow himself enough time to move the racket into the correct position for the preparation of the follow-up stroke.

After stating these general principles, it is very difficult to state which is the best method of serving as many of the leading players in the world have different techniques. What can be stated is that the shake hands grip players should experiment with the 'rotary' body action and the 'spring' action and try to incorporate the wrist action in the end product.

The return of service

Aims of the return of service

The return of a service is just as important as serving because if one cannot return well, then it usually means the point will be lost.

One can return a service in many ways. The way that you choose will often depend upon the type of player you are opposing. He may be left handed so special considerations may have to be taken into account; he may be exceptionally good on the forehand or the backhand; he may be weak at taking topspin. If you do not know your opponent's style then test him out as early as possible during the game. Although one may have the option of pushing, blocking, counter attacking, topspinning or backspinning a service, one should always concentrate on placing the ball so that the opponent becomes cramped in his style or he has to move quickly. Therefore concentrate on usually keeping the ball away from the centre area of the table and aim for a place within six inches of the end and/ or side lines and preferably going away from the opponent. Ideally, try to make the ball 'break' off the side of the table.

When making contact with the ball from the server one is trying to gain the initiative but this is not always possible. If there is so much backspin on the ball and it is so short that you do not feel safe in attempting to attack it, then use a push stroke and place it. However, you should always try to think of what return the opponent can make and how you can react. Therefore it is necessary to try and return the ball so that there is sufficient spin on it and it is so short in length that the opponent can only play it back without much of an attacking stroke.

Another alternative is to include speed on the push as well as spin so as to make the server hurry his second stroke and therefore give you the possible chance of gaining the initiative in the rally.

One should concentrate on being in the correct ready stance and one should aim for perfect balance and movement into the ball, with the muscles controlling the wrist joint and forearm not over-taut upon impact. The actual position in relation to the table will depend upon the player's ability and the opponent's style but the general rule for a player wishing to attack with his forehand is to be so positioned that a continuation of the backhand side line would dissect him. Always watch your opponent's position at the table; then decide if there is any possibility of him making a serve which you may not be able to receive effectively and if necessary move into a new position for the ready stance. An example of this is when playing a player who has been serving throughout the game from his backhand court and then suddenly moves across to the forehand court. You now know that he could well serve a fast ball down your forehand so you may feel insecure with your usual ready stance. You should therefore move to a new ready stance position so that your amount of movement will be reduced if he serves on your forehand. If however he does serve down your backhand it is still easy for you to play the ball diagonally to his backhand.

As the player is serving one should observe the descent of the opponent's racket and the movements just before contact, on contact, and finally on follow-through. The best method is by keeping a careful eye on the wrist movements. During flight try to assess the direction, spin and speed.

Footwork for the return of service

1. Attacking players who prefer to use forehand strokes.

In the initial stage some players prefer to stand a little further back and as the ball is about to make contact with the opponent's racket, they start moving forward with a short two footed skipping action into the ready stance position. Further movement should not occur until the ball is moving towards the player. Once he knows the ball is going to the back hand court then the left foot will move first but if it is going to the forehand court then the right foot should be first to move. Once the player has realised in what direction the ball is travelling, he must then decide if the service will he short or long as the length of the service will determine the direction of the second and third steps.

If the service comes short to the backhand court of the table then in the second foot movement the right foot will move forward. If the service comes long, the receiver could play a backhand stroke with his present footwork or move to play a forehand stroke.

When the service comes down the middle of the table with the second movement the left foot does not move towards the right foot but moves towards the backhand corner of the table and then the right foot moves forward or backwards depending on the length of the service. When the service comes down the forehand court of the table the left foot moves towards the right foot and then in the third step the right foot moves forward or backward depending on the length of the service.

If a right-handed player serves from the forehand court then the receiver will alter his ready stance. This ready stance is very similar to that of attacking players who favour backhand strokes, or players who are small in size and cannot use the other footwork.

2. Attacking players who have strong backhand strokes.

Although there is not so much movement involved with this type of footwork a player must be very careful not to be caught in a position where his feet are too far apart, otherwise he will experience difficulty in moving in the next required direction. The player will not receive the ball so often with his forehand in the backhand court because excessive movement will be involved. The first foot movement regarding the receive of service, follows the same general principles as the footwork for the receive of service by players who prefer to use forehand strokes. An exception is when the service comes down the middle of the table, the player then has an option of which foot to move first, depending on whether he wants to play a backhand or forehand stroke. If he wants to play a forehand, he moves his left foot first and for a backhand he will move his right foot first.

3. Defensive players

Defensive player's footwork for the receive of the short service is very similar to that of the attacking player who favours the stance nearer to the middle of the table. With the long services the following footwork could be used if the player wishes to use backspin strokes.

It is sometimes possible to anticipate the direction and length of the service so that the receiver can move early and therefore gain an advantage but this can be a very dangerous ploy especially if the server can conceal the direction of the service until the very last moment.

Younger players who are lacking in height and females who often lack the dynamic movement of the male are often encouraged to use the ready stance of a player who prefers to dominate with his forehand. Many players have suffered in the past because they have been coached in footwork which is not suitable to their physique or style of game. After the adolescent growth spurt, a player may be able to change to that of a forehand dominating player if his strength and height have increased.

Doubles

There are no doubles matches in the World or European Men's Team Championships, but the Women's Doubles match can often decide the outcome of the Women's Team Championships. In the World and European Men's Championships there are three players a side, each playing a maximum of three singles sets, and the first team to win five sets will win the match. However, in the World or European Women's Team Championships, there may be two, three or four players participating on one team. The match will consist of a maximum of four singles and one doubles set. An outstanding lady player on any one team can almost win the match entirely by herself, as she can play in three of the five sets.

The most important team matches for European players besides the championships previously mentioned are the European Super League matches. In this league, doubles sets account for two of the seven sets played. If a team can win the Men's Doubles and the Mixed Doubles they can gain overall victory by winning only two of the remaining five singles sets. Between 1974 and 1976 English teams usually won most of their doubles sets in the European League, with the pairings of Desmond Douglas and Denis Neale and Desmond Douglas and Linda Howard.

The Men's Doubles, Women's Doubles and Mixed Doubles competitions in major tournaments are coveted titles and are very prestigious for the players and their associations. Therefore, when choosing a doubles combination, whether for World, European or domestic events, selectors must realise that it is possible that their best two players at singles may not be as good a doubles partnership as another pair of lower-ranked players.

Players have contrasting styles and it is very difficult to state what is the best combination of styles for doubles play because much will depend upon the techniques of their opponents. When analysing successful doubles combinations in England, it is noticeable that there is a marked contrast in their playing styles. Desmond Douglas and Denis Neale can be classified as a counter attacking combination, whereas the partnership of Paul Day and Andrew Barden can be classified as a topspin loop drive combination. Jill Hammersley and Linda Howard form a defensive and counter attacking combination. In Europe, two of the most successful doubles combinations over the past seven years were Stellan Bengtsson and Kjell Johansson (Sweden), a topspin loop drive and counter attacking combination and Drautin Surbek and Anton Stipancic, a topspin loop drive combination.

A study of these Men's Doubles pairs shows that they all have a familiar characteristic of one player being right-handed and the other, left-handed The players also have very strong forehand topspin loop drives and/or forehand smashes. Usually the players with the stronger forehand topspin loop drives have weaker backhand strokes. This is because during a game of singles they have been coached to try and dominate the rallies with their stronger forehand strokes.

The big advantage of a right and left-handed doubles pair is that they find it easier to play a ball from the middle area of their side of the table, with their more powerful forehand strokes. Also, after they have played a *service* or stroke, they can usually move out to the same side of the table throughout the match and so leave the whole area behind the table free, for their partner to play the next stroke.

When two right-handed players or two left-handed players are partnering each other, they are more likely to be restricted in their movements about the table. The players may move in a sequence like the left-handed and right-handed combination', or they can move in a circular system, either clockwise or anticlockwise. Partners who prefer to serve and dominate with their backhand strokes are likely to move in a clockwise direction, whereas the partners who prefer to serve and dominate wit their forehand strokes usually move in an anti-clockwise direction.

These partnerships may be able to follow a set sequence of movement for most of the rallies, but it is quite possible that at some stage in the set they will have to improvise upon their original sequence.

Doubles combinations depend upon close communication between the players regarding the understanding of their partners' stroke production, mental attitude and movement patterns.

Although there are exceptions to the rules, two players who try to win the point very quickly in singles matches do not make a successful doubles combination. In all doubles pairings there should be a player who can consistently return the ball to the opponent's side of the table. This is usually the person who will create the 'opening' for his partner to win the point by a smash or topsin loop drive.

A very important factor in doubles play is that of knowing how your partner is going to react to various situations. You must know if he will become nervous in a big tournament, or in an important match, or when close near the end of a game. It may be that he does not play convincingly or that his body movements may be too tentative. In these situations it is important that you really understand his menial state both on and off the table so that you can have a good idea of how to help and encourage him so that he may regain composure and resume playing up to his potential.

Because the ball is being struck alternately by each player, the 'non-striking' partner must have a clear understanding of what spin his partner is imparting upon the ball so that when the opponent plays a return stroke he will be able to follow up with an effective counter stroke. The amount of spin that your partner imparts upon the ball may be completely different from that of a similar stroke from you. With plenty of match practice, the understanding of each others' strokes should increase.

Men's Doubles partnerships that depend entirely on defensive strokes are usually unsuccessful, especially against a good forehand topspin loop drive combination. This is because the attacking players have plenty of time to move into the correct position to play their strokes and to angle the ball very wide. If forehand topspin loop driving players can understand their partner's positional play, they should have plenty of time to move into position even against the counter attacking players, and if their spin variation and consistency of stroke is good then they should have a good chance of winning most of their matches. A Men's Doubles partnership of one defensive player and one attacking player is usually unsuccessful, especially against opponents who have good topspin loop drives and forehand smashes. The attacking pair often dominate the rallies and create difficulties for the opposing attacking player, who will end up blocking the ball during most of the rallies.

In the Mixed Doubles, combinations of defence and attack, and all defensive combinations, are usually unsuccessful because the opposing man of an attacking partnership can usually dominate the rallies. The most ideal partnerships are often composed of a man who has a good variation of services and a topspin loop drive, and a woman who has a good counter attacking game and can control the opponents' services and effectively block the topspin loop drive. Jacques Secretin and. Claude Bergeret (France), the 1977 World Champions, are a good example of this type of combination.

In Women's Doubles the above principles regarding doubles partnerships do not really apply.

Women usually lack the dynamic power of men so that attacking players cannot move about the table from one point to another so quickly. Therefore they do not always obtain a position to play continuous attacking strokes. They also do not have the same amount of power in the execution of their strokes. In Women's Doubles, therefore, an attacking-defensive or a totally defensive combination still have a good chance of being successful.

Before playing a doubles match, it is very important, as in singles, to analyse the opponents' style of play and then decide upon your tactics. It could be that your partner dislikes playing against a certain style that one of your opponents uses, so you then have to decide whether it is best for your partner to receive service from him In the first game or the second game. However, it may turn out that you have no choice in the matter, because if they win the option to serve, they may decide to give the service away and therefore choose to receive the service. If you do have the option either to serve or receive the service, then you must consider whether it is worth trying to catch the opponents cold' and get off to a good start by playing the apparently worst order in the first game and keep your best order until the second game and latter half of the third game. Alternatively you could play your best order in the first game and then hope to demoralise the opponents for the second game or have a good start in the third game, so leaving the opposition too big a deficit to make up when the order of serving is changed in the third game.

Many doubles partnerships help each other by using prearranged tactics. A simple example is that of dropping the non-racket arm below the table and making a sign to indicate what service you are going to do. Some partnerships use the sign of two fingers pointing towards the floor as meaning a sidespin topspin service, or a clenched fist which means a sidespin backspin service. This advance information can help the partner prepare for the type of return the opponent is likely to play.

During a doubles game most of the tactics in singles matches still apply. Each player should try strokes during the game that assist his partner to dominate the game. While playing your strongest strokes, you should also try to play on the opponents' weakest strokes. A good tactic is that of quickly playing the ball towards the person who last played the ball, because it means he will have to move out of the way very quickly. If he is slow in moving, then it is likely that his partner will not be in a good position to play a 'point winning' stroke. When this situation occurs, the opponents often leave a large area of their court 'open' so that you can gain the intitiative in dictating the placement of the ball during the rally.

For a player to derive any enjoyment, feeling of participation, satisfaction or ultimate success from a ball game, be it cricket, tennis, badminton or t[illegible] tennis, it is vital to be able to hit a moving ball. [illegible] many people, this is a simple and intuitive act requiring no guidance or support at all. For others without a natural sense of coordination, it can be a nightmare. Before looking at ways in which hand-to-eye coordination can be nurtured and improved, the way in which the bat is held needs to be considered.

The grip

In a sense, there is only one way to hold a table tennis bat and that is with the grip that feels most comfortable for the player. Unfortunately, this simple rule does not always produce a grip which is suited to playing the game well. With the chosen grip it should be possible to make an instantaneous, fine adjustment to the angle of the bat to control the direction of the ball. There should be no need to after the grip between the forehand and backhand sides during a rally as table tennis is too fast a game to allow for this sort of luxury. As a result there are two established grips, the 'shakehold', preferred by most European and Western players and the 'penhold' adopted by many Asian players.

The 'shakehold' grip is achieved by literally shaking hands with the handle of the bat. The forefinger should be placed on the bottom part of the backhand side of the blade, and the thumb should rest on the centre part of the forehand side near to the neck of the handle. The remaining three fingers wrap firmly, but not too tightly, around the handle. A useful tip for judging whether the grip is too tight is to check the whiteness of the knuckles. If they are white then the player clearly needs to relax the grip or control of movement will be inhibited. This type of grip may initially feel awkward to the beginner who may well want to adjust it in some way. It's important, though, to keep correcting a bad grip because it can lead to untold difficulties at a later stage.

'Penhold' is also a very apt description for the second of the two most popular grips in the game. Here the thumb and forefinger close around the neck of the bat handle at the point where it meets the blade, in much the same way in which you might hold a pen. The remaining fingers can either be splayed across the other side of the blade or alternatively cupped. The distinguishing feature of the penhold grip is that only one side of the bat is used throughout to hit the ball.

Because of this, bats designed exclusively for players using the penhold grip are available with rubber covering one side of the bat and an ergonomic handle. On balance the shakehold grip is probably the easier of the two grips to master as it gives the most flexibility. Nevertheless, it's worth bearing in mind that there are millions of Chinese youngsters learning with the penhold type of grip every day, and it is China which has been a dominating force in the game since the early 1960s.

Although both grips appear very different from one another, they both have one important thing in common. The thumb and the forefinger are positioned in such a way as to enable delicate and instant control to be exercised over the angle of the bat throughout play.

Coordination

There are a couple of quick and simple tests which a coach can use to gauge whether a player is coordinated, and these can be performed without having to pick up a bat or ball, Rubbing the stomach with one hand and patting the head with the other at the same time is one useful exercise; swinging the arms in big circles from the shoulders with one arm going in one direction and the other arm in the opposite direction is another, The proficiency with which these tasks are performed can be a good indication of the likely level of coordination, However, do not write off an individual who appears at first sight to be awkward and clumsy as this does not always mean he will not make a useful player.

Hand-to-eye coordination, touch and early ball skills can be developed by one or two simple off-the-table exercises. The most obvious of these is bouncing the ball on the bat, which is also a useful opportunity to introduce and establish the correct grip. This exercise can be slowly developed in a progressive way to enhance the control of the would-be player over the moving ball. The next stage would be to:

- Bounce the ball at a consistent height
- Bounce the ball at a consistent height on the backhand of the bat
- Alternate bounces between the two sides
- Introduce the bouncing of the ball on the blade edge of the bat into any of these exercises.

As well as the ability to coordinate the hand and react to the continually varying movement of the ball, Judging where and when to make contact, the player also needs to gain control over the force with which it is struck. A simple and effective way of isolating this particular aspect of ball control is to practise volleying the ball repeatedly against a wall. Unlike a squash ball which is comparatively, soft and lacks a high degree of bounce, table tennis balls are quite the opposite. In this exercise you will discover that it does not require much force for the ball to rebound too fast for the average beginner to make a successful second or third shot.

From the coach's point of view, a valuable piece of information emerges from these simple exercises. Ball control is easier when the bat, and therefore the ball, is kept close to the head and upper body. Conversely it becomes progressively more difficult to perform as the playing arm becomes extended and the bat is held further away. This is a useful factor to bear in mind when the first attempts at play on the table take place.

Before we look at the four strokes which form the basis of the game as it exists today, it's worth considering the principles involved in strokeplay: in other words, the key elements in producing a shot which constitute good technique. In table tennis this is usually broken down into seven separate areas, which are common to virtually every shot in the game. They are:

1. Stance
2. Table position
3. Length
4. Timing
5. Body action
6. Bat arm and bat angle
7. Free arm.

To identify faults or weaknesses in technique, it is essential that a coach fully appreciates the part played by each of these factors. Together they form the 'magnificent seven' an invaluable checklist which can be used as a comprehensive way of analyzing a player's technique.

Stance

Considering that an incorrect stance is at the root of many players' problems, it's surprising how little attention is paid by coaches to this crucial feature. Table tennis is a fast one-to-one game with little time for recovery between shots. It makes sense then that the stance adopted should allow the player to move efficiently, at speed, to various parts of the table and at the same time maintain good balance, steady vision and control over the stroke.

The optimum stance for table tennis is shown in the diagram opposite. Working from the feet upwards, the significant points to bear in mind are that:

- The feet are spread as wide apart as the shoulders,
- The knees are bent slightly and projected inwards a little so that the weight of the body shifts to the balls of the feet at the front instep. This enables the player to spring quickly from side to side.
- The upper body is arched forward so that there is space between the bat arm and the lower chest to enable arm movement to be unrestricted. A good tip is to check that the chin is about in line vertically with the knees.
- Both arms are held with an angle of about 90 degrees at the elbow.
- The player's position when playing the ball, which changes throughout the duration of the rally, should always be what is termed 'relative to the line of play'. With the exception, possibly of one or two of the more advanced defensive shots, this is invariably square to the line of play. A simple way to illustrate this is to point out that after the shot is

played, the player's shoulders and chest should end up facing the direction in which the ball is hit. The feet will also be pointing in the same direction, roughly in line with the shoulders.

A final word on stance. It's impossible to be definitive about the precise angle of the bend of the knees or to what degree the upper body should be crouched forward or the exact width to which the feet should be apart. All these factors will be affected by the height of the individual in question. It will be of little help to the youngster who can barely peer over the table to insist that he keeps his feet as wide apart as his shoulders. This will only make his stance problem worse, so a coach should use his intelligence, be flexible and make allowances for the individual. If you are dealing with a seven-foot giant, instruct him to widen his base beyond the width of the shoulders so that lie can focus better on the ball.

Table position

It helps youngsters learning the game to maintain a position which is relatively close to the table. Not only does it help give them a good timing point but it is also a bit easier to hit accurately into the target area which, for most newcomers, will simply be the other side of the net. The further away from the table, the harder this becomes. The ideal distance is probably the point, once the correct stance has been adopted, where the bat is barely touching the edge of the table,

Length

In the initial stages of learning the game, the swing of the playing arm should be kept short. A long swing makes it harder to keep control over the speed and direction of the ball. The length and swing of any shot can be broken down into three distinct phases: the time when the bat is accelerating in the swing, the point at which contact is made with the ball and, lastly, the follow-through when the bat arm is slowing down.

Not only is a short swing necessary, but it is important to bear in mind that the main part of the stroke probably 70 per cent of the energy exerted should be devoted to the acceleration phase. A player hitting the ball too early in the swing will have difficulty later in learning to generate power to hit the ball hard.

Timing

Some players, picking up a bat for the first time, will instinctively want to hit the ball late in its bounce. They find it hard to do otherwise, because they feel they need time to react and think about the shot before striking the ball. You often find that this type of individual makes a good defensive player in which the bulk of their game is played some distance away from the table.

However, unless the player feels totally uncomfortable, you should try and teach 'peak of the bounce' timing. The main benefit to be gained from hitting the ball at the highest point of the bounce is that at this point the greatest part of the target area, that is, the other side of the net, becomes available.

As the ball drops away from its peak, it becomes more difficult to hit down on to the other side. What inevitably happens is that the player tries to compensate by hitting underneath the ball and lobbing it up in the hope that it lands somewhere on the other side. Alternatively, there is a tendency to curve and brush the ball, to try and make it loop up and dip down over the net.

Body action

It's a popular misconception that the only pan of the body that gains any exercise value from table tennis is the playing arm. This is nonsense! Any top player will tell you that the whole of the body is utilized in a match. Even with the basic strokes in the game, you will soon appreciate the contribution that the legs, waist and shoulders make in developing, for example, a hard, aggressive forehand drive.

Bat arm and bat angle

We have already touched on the way in which ball control is affected as the bat arm becomes more extended. It is important when you come to introduce a new stroke that you are aware, for example, of the best angle at which the elbow should be held for maximum effect.

You should consider the bat arm in much the same way as you might regard a whip. Each of its three joints contributes in a different way. The shoulder is like the handle of a whip and although it doesn't move fast, it is the source of the power which will ultimately be transmitted to the bat. The elbow moves slightly faster but lacks the strength and power of the shoulder. The wrist is the head of the whip and the fastest moving part of the arm but, equally, it is the weakest. All three joints need to be fluid, synchronized and working in such a way that they complement each other.

A further factor which will have a critical influence on whether the ball clears the net and lands on the other side of the table, is the angle at which the bat is held. This can either be 'open' or 'closed' as illustrated opposite.

Free arm

This is the last of the seven points on our checklist. Proper use of the free arm helps the rotation of the body, particularly in the power shots. Its greatest contribution as far as the beginner is concerned, however, is in helping to coordinate the process of stroke production and connecting bat with ball. By using the free arm as a sort of gun sight to point at the ball, it can often make all the difference between hitting and missing.

Footwork and reaction

Table tennis is a fast game played over a small area. It's easy for beginners to fall into the trap of stretching and reaching for the ball instead of moving the feet and body. But, like all bad habits, it becomes a hard one to kick at a later stage. It doesn't matter what stroke we are talking about, they are all that much easier to perform if the body is in the right position in relation to the ball. So what are the main factors that affect a player's ability, to move efficiently" No doubt there are plenty of scientific explanations which answer the question. The short answer though is that there are three as far as table tennis is concerned:

1. Footwork
2. Stability and balance
3. Weight transference.

We will look at the various types of *footwork* used in the game at a later stage in this chapter. Suffice it to say that there are two different patterns of footwork, each of which is used in its own way to respond to the typical situations that most players find themselves in during a game.

Stability also affects movement. The need to make allowances for the physical characteristics of the player has also been mentioned. To recap, the ground rules to bear in mind with the stances are:

- A stance where the base is too narrow and the body is upright usually impedes the player's ability to keep good balance.
- A stance which is too wide and squat is very stable, but quick movement after a shot has been played is made very difficult.

Somewhere between the two lies the best stance for your player and it is usually the point where the centre of gravity is just above the base of the spine.

Weight transference is a technical expression which recognizes that there are several shots which require the player to transfer the body's weight from one foot to the other. This is particularly true of the forehand drive and all its related strokes. It is also especially important in the process of generating power and speed. The player has to be capable of transferring his body weight when moving to one side of the table or the other between strokes.

In terms of the player's development, the fundamentals of good economical footwork should be taught as soon as possible, preferably at the same time as the four basic strokes.

There are essentially two types of *footwork* used in the modem game, 'stepping footwork' and 'running footwork'. For the beginner, the former is the most appropriate. Stepping footwork is used close to the table and its main feature is that the feet do not cross one another. It's virtually a sideways, skipping movement which allows the player to maintain a solid stance and makes recovery easy once the shot is played. If the feet should cross when close up to the table, it's hard for players to recover stability especially if forced to move across to the other side of the table for the next ball. Running footwork, on the other hand, is used further away from the table over a larger area. As its name suggests, it involves the feet and legs crossing each other in a normal running fashion. Because the player is away from the table, there is a little more time to effect recovery for the next ball.

Regular footwork

The main challenge facing a coach when trying to instil correct, but nimble, footwork in a player is to reach a stage where a footwork pattern becomes almost automatic. The player no longer has to think how and where to move the feet because it has become an instinctive process. We do this by using what is known as 'regular footwork exercises'. These are practices at the table, where the player knows in advance where the ball is going to be placed, for example, a series of forehand drives played alternately from the backhand and forehand wings of the table. Depending on natural talent and ability, the player eventually reaches a stage where the one or two steps involved become an almost unconscious process which should be repeated automatically in a game situation. Here ate a few regular footwork exercises you might try in your practice sessions.

Alternate forehand and backhand drives to a backhand block

This is played using the same diagonal. The main point to watch out for is that the player is shifting between a square and side to square stance. This exercise can be varied so that the forehand is played from the forehand wing to introduce a sideways, skipping movement as well. Make sure, though, that the weight is on the back foot and is being transferred through to the front when the forehand is being played.

Alternate forehand and backhand drives to a forehand block

This is very similar to Exercise I but the backhand needs to be played from a very square position to ensure that the ball is returned to the opponent's forehand wing. It can also be varied in the same way as Exercise diagonally across the table.

Irregular footwork exercises

A quick indication of whether a footwork pattern has been, grooved into a player's subconscious is to test its effectiveness with an 'irregular' footwork exercise. This is an exercise which involves a switch in the direction of the ball at a point in the rally unknown to the player. It closely resembles a matchplay situation where the pace and direction of the ball will vary constantly during the rally. For example, using the backhand diagonal, the player hits a forehand drive to the opponent's backhand block. However, the opponent may switch any one of these balls down the forehand wing at any time.

All the regular footwork exercises describe earlier can quite easily be adjusted slightly so that the become irregular. Irregular footwork exercises can be enhanced one stage further so that once the direction of the ball has been switched, both players then have the freedom to play the point out much as they might do in a match.

You may well find that the transition from regular to irregular practices is not without its snags. Some players can demonstrate beautiful footwork patterns if the practice involves the use of regular footwork.

A combination exercise with both players hitting alternate forehand and backhand drives.

One player will always be playing across the table with the other playing down the line. This is a more advanced regular footwork exercise but should not be beyond the capability of most novices. But, as with any practice routine, if the players are spending most of their time picking the ball off the floor, then the exercise is too difficult. Go back to something easier and more manageable.

The three Rs—reading, reacting and recovering

We are all born with different levels of natural ability and we all differ in the speed with which we are able to react to situations. The reason why some players seem to be in the right position almost before the ball has been struck is that their natural sense of anticipation is razor sharp. Although good anticipation is a gift you are born with, it can be improved upon simply by reading the other player's game and recovering to the best position in time for the next ball.

How often do you hear that immortal line 'Watch the ball!'? It's true, watching the ball is important but as far as table tennis is concerned, this expression should really be 'Watch the player!' By watching the opponent's body action and, in particular the opponent's bat, it is possible to pick up clues and read where the ball is likely to be hit. If a player is 'ball watching' and not 'player watching' it's likely that the necessary reaction is only going to occur when the ball is perhaps halfway across the net on its journey back. By watching the opponent's bat immediately before the ball is played, some slight advantage can be gained and his return shot can be gained and his return shot can be understood a split second earlier. In the final analysis, this can mean the difference between always being on the defensive or instead being in a position to seize the initiative.

Service and receive

An outsider watching a game of local league table tennis could be forgiven for thinking that the service is simply a means of putting the ball into play. Even at quite high levels of domestic competition, it is often difficult to draw any other impression. This is a great shame because, like tennis, the service has grown in significance in recent years to the point where it would not be all understatement to say that it is now the most important stroke.

At what other point in the game does a player have the opportunity to exercise complete control over the ball? A good service can win a point outright, it can open up the rally for an attacking shot, it can deceive the opponent and in some cases, it can even become a psychological threat to the receiver. You only have to look at the way in which the Chinese, and now several of the top European teams, have come to exploit its potential to realize what a valuable weapon it can be. It makes good sense to impress upon any newcomer the advantages to be gained from being able to serve well. It doesn't mean that they have to be able to impart fantastic amounts of spin. Just simply that they are capable of delivering a tight, economical service which is strong enough to prevent the opponent from gaining an advantage.

The service laws

Because the service has been delivered in so many innovative and dramatic ways in the past, the ITTF has been forced to legislate on a number of successive occasions on the manner in which it should be delivered. In the 1950s when sponge rubber first came on to the scene, several of its earl exponents started to gain what was seen as an unfair advantage by spinning the ball with their fingers prior to actually serving it, In the late seventies many combination bat players took to hiding the bat from the opponent's view by concealing it under the table immediately prior to the service. By doing this they gained a great deal of deception because the opponent would be unaware until the very last minute which side of the bat would be used to strike the ball and, therefore, whether it would be spinning or not. Other players hid both the ball and bat from view by standing with their backs to both the opponent and the umpire, turning only at the last second at the point of contact with the ball. Umpires, therefore, now pay very close attention to whether a service conforms with the laws of the game. It is important that beginners should be aware of these laws and that they are capable of delivering a service which is not only effective but also legal and correct. The main rules to bear in mind are that:

- The service begins with the ball resting on the palm of the free hand which should be above the table, stationary and flat with the fingers together and the thumb free.
- The bat should begin the service action from above the table.
- The ball should be thrown upwards at least 16 centimetres.
- The ball should be struck on its descent, from behind the white baseline. It should bounce once on the server's side of the table before crossing the net.
- The service should at all times be clearly visible to the umpire.

Learning to serve

It is by no means easy for a beginner to coordinate all the actions that go into the service routine and at the same time stay within the laws of the game. A step-by-step approach is often the best way of achieving this and you might want to try the following method.

1. Start by getting the player used to holding the ball still in the palm of the hand without it rolling around. This is a common difficulty and it can be easily overcome by making the palm of the hand into a very shallow Cup by slightly bending the knuckles.

2. Now move on to the throw tip. To make sure the ball is being thrown upwards in a consistent vertical path, ask the player to position the bat directly beneath the free hand. A good throw up should result in the ball landing on the centre of the bat held directly below.

3. Next, instead of simply letting the ball bounce on the bat from the throw up, encourage the player to swing the bat a little as the ball is descending, hitting it up and forward over the net to bounce on the receiver's side. You might find the easiest way to introduce this stage is to adapt an existing technique, like the backhand push. If necessary, let the player lean over the table and gradually take the point of contact with the ball closer towards the baseline and finally just behind the baseline.
4. The last stage of the process is to adjust the swing a little so that the ball is being struck downwards making it bounce once on the server's side of the net before ultimately bouncing on the receiver's side.

It is important at all the stages outlined above that the bat is not being held too tightly. This will only restrict the player's ability to control the length of the service.

What makes a safe service a good service?

Top players spend hours and hours serving endless balls across the table in a bid to perfect their serving technique. But, irrespective of experience or ability, there are a number of basic points that all players need to know and practise in order to coordinate the body actions involved to perform a basic legal service.

Many new players complain that the ball bounces too high when they serve, thereby giving the receiver the opportunity to drive it hard back at them. Others complain that they are unable to control the length of their services which vary constantly.

Let's examine the first point. The main factor influencing the height to which the ball bounces is the height at which contact between bat and ball is made in relation to the table. If the server is hitting the ball at say, 30 centimetres or so above the table, then the ball will bounce at almost the same height over the net. Ideally, players should be encouraged to make contact at roughly the same height as the net or somewhere between 15 and 20 centimetres.

Next, the question of the length of serve. Short, medium, and long services all have their place in today's game. Where the ball bounces on the receiver's side of the table depends to a great extent on where it is placed on the server's own side. For a short service, the ball should be played close to the net on the server's own side. A medium length service requires the ball to be played mid table, and a long service is most easily achieved when the ball is played close to the server's own baseline, if it is to bounce at an equivalent point on the receiver's side of the table.

Another factor to bear in mind when looking at the length of the service is the angle of the bat. For a short or medium length service, make sure that it moves downwards, brushing the underside of the ball. By doing this, an element of backspin will be imparted, making it that little bit more awkward for the receiver to create an opening with an attacking shot.

For a longer service, the bat needs to be closed a little, making contact with the back of' the ball. Probably the most utilized service in the modern game is a short to medium length service down the centre of the table, directed at the receiver's playing shoulder. This has come to be known as the 'two bounce serve'.

In other words, if there was no one to return the ball, it would bounce twice on the receiver's side with the second bounce on or about the baseline. The length and direction are just about right to make it difficult for the opponent to decide in the first instance whether to play a forehand or backhand shot and secondly, whether to simply push the ball back, or try to drive or flick it instead. With this length of service, it is also quite possible for the server to put a useful amount of sidespin on the ball which only adds to the receiver's problems.

Receiving the serve

Let us turn our attention now to the other side of the equation, that of returning or receiving the service. From a beginner's point of view there are, essentially three points to consider:

- The stance and position of the receiver in relation to the server.
- How best to move to the ball, particularly when it is served short.
- What type of stroke to use to make the most effective return.

At no other point in the game does a correct stance become more vital. Make sure then, that the player is positioned square to the server, poised ready and alert to move swiftly into action. The bat should be pointing at the ball. Remind him that inevitably the server's bat is going to make contact with the ball so there is no need to waste time following the throw-up of the ball. Just keep the eyes firmly fixed on the bat.

The position of the receiver will depend to a large

extent from where the ball is being served. If it is coming from well over on the server's forehand side, then the receiver needs to be aware of the possible angles of play that need to be covered. In general terms, at least 50 to 60 per cent of play needs to be covered by the forehand, more so if the receiver has a useful forehand.

Long serves can be covered using the sort of stepping footwork. As far as short or medium length serves are concerned, the golden rule is to move the nearest foot to the bounce of the ball. This should bring the head and body sufficiently close to the ball to enable good control to be exerted.

Lastly, the type of stroke to use will very much depend on the length and type of spin on the ball. A short backspin service is best received with a short delicate push over the net with the ball being taken just before the peak of its bounce. Make sure that the bat is not being gripped too tightly so that the desired level of touch is not lost. The medium or two bounce service can be returned with what is referred to as the flick taking the ball at its peak and hitting it deep into the server's side of the table. This is similar in principle to the two basic drive shots. The real difference is that it is played with a short arm where the wrist is the main moving joint, rotating quickly in a 'flicked' fashion over the back of the ball.

Long services should be dealt with using the forehand drive. By keeping the ball deep and into the server's body, it narrows the angle of play available. All these types of receive have one thing in common; they are positive. If the receiver dithers over the return it is a sure fire way of getting into difficulty.

Practising the service and receive

It is not easy for the coach to create practice situations which concentrate on the service and receive, without boredom on the part of the pupils quickly setting in. You need to be varied and imaginative but here are one or two exercises you might like to try. In the long run, though, hours of dedicated practice on the service, in particular, can pay handsome dividends and literally put points on a player's game almost overnight.

Exercise 1

The server serves five short backhand services and then five short forehand services into boxes 1,2,3 and 4. The services should be short enough so that they would be capable of bouncing twice on the receiver's side.

The receiver pushes the service into boxes I and 2 back into box 8, and then serves into boxes 3 and 4 into box 7.

The server then serves five long backhand services and then five long forehand services into box 5. The receiver returns each one into box 9, preferably by using a forehand drive.

Total 50 services

Exercise 2

The server plays 50 services at random into the five boxes shown on the diagram. The receiver tries to return as many as possible deep into box 9 using attacking shots wherever possible.

Both these exercise can be made 'fun' games. For example, if the server fails to hit any of the prescribed targets over the course of 50 services, each miss counts

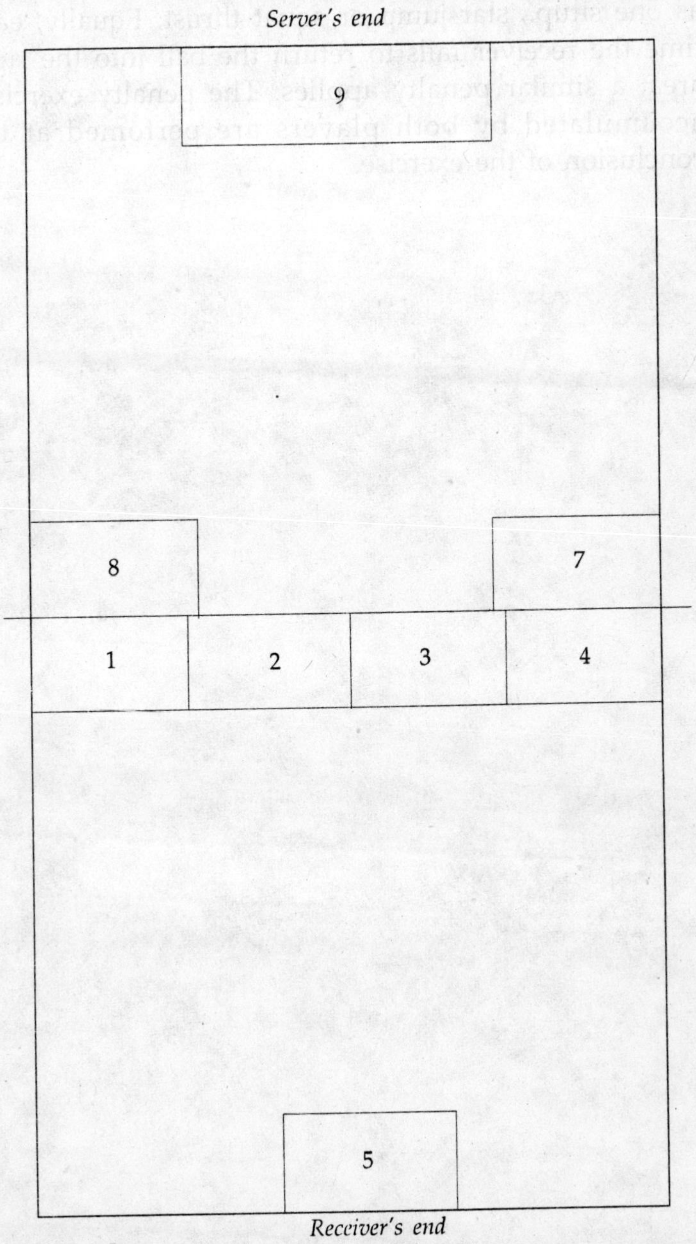

Server's end

9

8

7

1

2

3

4

5

Receiver's end

Exercise I

as one situp., star jump or squat thrust. Equally, each time the receiver fails to return the ball into the right area, a similar penalty applies. The penalty exercises accumulated by both players are perfomed at the conclusion of the exercise.

5

TECHNIQUES

The path to becoming a top player follows a route which becomes progressively steeper the further you travel. Rest assured, bad habits and basic flaws will have the same effect as trying to climb the Eiger with holes in your boots! The message we are trying to get across is a simple one: time spent on acquiring strong basic skills is time well spent. As you will find out, virtually all the more advanced shots are derived from four simple strokes which in turn are all based on the same fundamental principles. If you get the foundations right, there's every chance of you building a respectable game which should enable you to fulfil your potential.

Back in the Forties and Fifties, there were umpteen different styles of grip being used at international level. Variations still exist today but they are generally much more subtle than in former years. Some things never change though, and essentially there will only ever be two ways of holding a table tennis bat with a good grip or with a bad grip. A bad grip is one which is uncomfortable, which limits flexibility, inhibits the execution of certain strokes, or needs changing between the forehand and backhand wings. A good grip suffers none of these drawbacks but acts as a natural extension of the playing hand. It may vary in appearance from one player to the next, but this will be because each player has found precisely the position which serves him or her the best.

The type of grip preferred by most Western and European players is known as the *shakehand* grip. It is achieved by literally shaking hands with the handle of the bat and is characterized by the forefinger being extended along the base of the blade and the thumb resting on the opposite side. The remaining three fingers surround the handle and the shoulder of the bat should be sitting neatly under that area of skin that lies between thumb and forefinger, Try not to cock your wrist but instead let it drop slightly so the upper edge of the bat lies at roughly the same height as your wrist joint.

One of the great advantages of the shalkehand grip is that it allows for instant delicate adjustments to be made to the angle of the bat during play. This fine degree of control is made possible because of the positioning of the thumb and forefinger. As you will soon discover, control over bat and hand is absolutely critical in this game and it will be lost if you make the mistake of gripping the bat too tightly.

It would be wrong not to mention the other most popular grip in the game, not least because it is favoured by half the population of China, the greatest table-tennis nation on earth. This is the *penhold* grip, so called because the handle is gripped by the thumb and forefinger in much the same way as you might hold a pen. The remaining fingers either rest or are spread across the opposite side of the bat, which, unlike the shakehand grip, is not used to strike the ball.

Uncomfortable though it might appear, the penhold grip has been used to tremendous effect by many great world champions. Why is it that some players look as though !hey have all the time in the world yet others are failing over themselves even to get near the ball? Unfortunately, there is no simple answer to this puzzle it depends on many factors and variables such as natural skill, talent and co-ordination. But there are a few key principles which, it mastered properly, will help you on your way to international acclaim.

Stance

The right sort of stance will give you a sound base to operate from. It needs to be one that will help you sustain balance, transfer your bodyweight, keep a steady vision and let You spring quickly and economically to all corners of the table. Start with your feet about as wide as your shoulders. Keep you knees bent slightly and stick your backside out a little, Crouch forward by arching your back so that your chin is in line vertically with your knees. Make sure that your playing arm is held out in front of you with the elbow bent and its movement unrestricted by your Upper body. Your bat should be just about grazing the edge of the table. Your free arm, which is a vital ingredient in keeping an overall balance, should be held parallel to the playing arm.

Lastly, make sure that at all times your weight is on the balls of your feet and not on your heels. If you've managed to copy correctly all the points just described, you'll probably find that this is precisely where your body weight is being supported. As you read on, you will notice that we use the term 'peak of the bounce' on many occasions. Developments in the game over the last ten years or so have shown us that, for many shots, this is undoubtedly the optimum timing point. It usually occurs at a point which is above net height, and because of this the target area is made bigger, it is easier to make full use of your power and it gives your opponent less time to respond.

If you try to adopt a 'peak of the bounce' timing point from Day One, it should stop with you for the rest of your playing career This should prove useful when you get involved in a high-pressure game, instead of being forced away from the table and thereby hitting the ball later, your intuition and instinct will be telling you to stop up there and fight it out in fine attacking style.

Not everyone is successful in acquiring this habit. Some players discover that they need more time to execute their strokes properly, and therefore they prefer to take the ball a little later. For this reason, players whose natural timing point is after the peak, or late, tend to become defenders and adopt the backspin game. This is no bad thing you only have to look at the top Korean, Lee Gun San, to realize that there is still a place on the international circuit for this style of play.

Stay square!

The way you position your body in relation to where you intend to hit the ball is a major factor which will enable you to glide easily between shots.

Ideally, you should be finishing most of your strokes with your shoulders and chest facing the point to which you are hitting the ball, known in the trade as 'square to the line of play'. To help you achieve this, your feet should also be pointing towards this same area. Gone are the days of Victor Barna when everything was 'side on', as it is in tennis. Because of the speed of today's game, you simply haven't got the time to indulge in such luxury.

Don't forget, though, that during a rally there are so many different variables at work, not least your opponent, his position, the ball, its speed, spin, and direction and your own state of readiness. It may not always be possible to get into exactly the right position, but nevertheless this should still be your aim.

Don't be just a ballwatcher!

What separates the great from the not-so-great in this game is the gift of anticipation. Those who have it are the game's clairvoyants, and seemingly can guess the future and known where the ball is going before you've even hit it, Sweden's Jan Ova Waldner and England's own Desmond Douglas are obvious examples. The rest of us are mere mortals who live in the present, missing chances and losing matches.

However, one of the reasons why some players remain mere mortals is that they only watch the ball. They could, if they applied themselves, elevate their status by developing their sense of anticipation.

Watching the ball alone means you react far too late. Watching the opponent, on the other hand, and in particular his bat as well as the ball will provide vital clues about what is going to happen. This will give you that miniscule but nevertheless crucial bit of extra time which allows you to react earlier and help you seize the initiative.

In the modern game, there is a core of four basic strokes which form the basis of every shot. They are:

1. the backhand push.
2. the forehand drive.
3. the backhand drive.
4. the forehand push.

From the drive strokes come all the topspin shots and their variations. From the push strokes comes the backspin or defensive, chopping style of play, You may well find that you have a greater aptitude for, say, the driving style than the pushing style, but don't think this excuses you from the need to master thoroughly all four. Only after this stage has been reached should your natural inclinations be allowed to give your game an identity.

Backhand push

With all the pushing and chopping strokes, the bat needs to be held in what we term an open angle, in this case using the backhand side of the blade.

Start by facing the direction you want to play the ball—remember, square to the line of play—with your feet in line with your shoulders. Neither foot should be in front of the other. You should be close to the table but not leaning over it. The ball is played from directly in front of, or just to the left of your stomach, and under your chin. If the ball is moving wide, shift across to this position first before you start the shot.

Now, using just your elbow, move your bat forwards on a downward trajectory and stroke the back of the ball at the peak of its bounce, Your elbow should be at about an angle of ninety degrees as you make contact, Your follow-through should be smooth and short but not jerky or you will lose control over the length of shot. The backhand push, just like its forehand counterpart, is a soft delicate stroke used to control the ball at the beginning of a rally and to prevent the opponent from gaining any advantage. It should be played short and in such a way that the ball almost caresses the net as it glides across the table.

A good way of retaining maximum control over flight and direction is to keep your head close to the bounce of the ball as you perform the stroke. At the same time, use your free arm to point to the ball as an aid to co-ordination. Length is determined largely by making sure that your forearm and grip are suitably relaxed. If you find the ball is bouncing too high when it hits the other side of the table, check that you aren't hitting under it. This might be due to your bat angle which could be too open, thereby lifting the ball as you strike it. You will probably find that the optimum bat angle is around forty-five degrees off the vertical.

Avoid using your wrist at this early stage. The wrist becomes enormously important later when we come to look at spinning the ball. All the arm joints have a part to play in stroke production. In certain strokes, like the push, one joint, in this case the elbow, assumes the lead role, in other shots, like the forehand topspin, all three joints from the shoulder downwards must synchronize together to produce the finished article.

Its not too difficult to set up a series of table exercises which involve using only backhand push. The diagrams give you one or two examples to start with. Once you feel that you've mastered the basic principles of the technique, concentrate on achieving consistency in distance, height and direction.

Forehand drive

We deliberately started with the backhand push because it's usually regarded as the easiest to learn of the four basic strokes. But there are no hard and fast rules which govern the order in which you gather your basic armoury of shots. There's a strong school of thought which takes the view that all novice players should learn to drive the ball before learning to push it. The rationale for this lies in the theory that, under pressure, you will keep your aggressive instincts, because driving and hitting the ball is the first thing you learnt all those years ago.

At certain times during a game, you will be presented with balls on which you must make a snap decision to push or to drive. The push will keep the ball safe but it's a negative sort of shot in this situation and 'It probably won't win you the point outright. The drive, on the other hand, represents a more positive approach, it's a bit more risky but only fractionally so and will undoubtedly give you a better chance of winning the rally. Only through practice will you find out what suits you best.

Let's turn our attention to the shot itself. The same principles of *finishing up* square to the line of play still apply, but with the forehand drive it usually helps if you start the stroke with a stance which is partly side-to-square. If you're a right-handed player, you should be leading a little with the left foot.

Make sure that your bat is being held with a slightly closed angle and your elbow is at about ninety degrees and at least 13 cm away from your body. Think in terms of rolling a large hula-hoop along the road. Using your shoulder, move your bat forwards and upwards at the same time, hitting through the back of the ball at the peak of its bounce. Your bat should finish its follow-through roughly in line with your nose. To enable you to do this, your upper body should be rotating slightly from a side-to-square position to finish the stroke square. As a reminder, it sometimes helps if you gently grasp your playing wrist with your free arm as you're performing the stroke, This will have the effect of automatically pulling and rotating your upper body through to the finishing position.

At the same time, and as if you haven't got enough to think about already, your weight should be transferring from the back foot through to the leading, front foot. Its important to establish this principle of weight transference early on because it plays such an integral part at a later stage when you want to put power and speed into your game and be able to hit the ball harder.

When you first practise the forehand drive, use the forehand diagonal of the table to start with. The diagonals are the longest sections of the table and give you a greater margin of error to allow you to get the distance right. Remember, you should be hitting at the peak of the bounce with the ball clearly travelling in a downwards path to the other side of the net. If you find that you're overhitting the end of the table, it could be because you are leaning back without realizing it. It this is so, it means that your bat angle will be wrong, resulting in your hitting under instead of over the ball.

What happens if the ball is wide? Answer 'I stick my bat out and try to reach it.' Wrong! You don't reach in this game, not unless you are in dire trouble. Instead, you reposition yourself by moving your feet.

This shouldn't be a problem because by this stage you'll have got yourself into the habit of keeping to a good stance which allows you to spring around quite effortlessly.

Backhand drive

At one time, it was possible for players to reach quite a high level in the game a world ranking, even—largely on the strength of a powerful forehand drive and topspin. Their backhand only needed to be a containing stroke, and when an opening occurred on the backhand wing they would run around and put the ball away with their forehand. Then, in the mid-Seventies, along came a new breed of players led predominantly by the Hungarians and the Swedes, who were strong on both wings and who could apply virtually the same amount of power and spin with their backhand as with their forehands. The forehand-only experts quickly disappeared from view, outmanoeuvred and outplayed by their more versatile successors. If you wish to achieve any degree of success, it is important that you also become strong on both wings,

Your approach to the stroke should be the same as for the backhand push square and facing the area of the table in which you wish the ball to land. Make sure you don't lead with your right foot as this will make it difficult for you to shift across to your forehand wing. Unlike the push, though, this shot is played over the ball so a slightly closed bat angle is required.

With your elbow at an angle of about ninety degrees move the bat forwards and upwards by using your elbow joint, starting from a point which is just to the left of your stomach. As you make contact again, at the top of the bounce try and let your wrist turn over the ball. The important point to bear in mind, is that the power for the backhand drive comes from the elbow; the wrist serves only as a finishing touch to guide the ball onto the right flightpath, which will be a downward trajectory. You might find it helpful to think of the stroke as trying to punch the ball with your knuckles but using only your forearm to do it.

For maximum control, keep your head over the ball and avoid reaching and therefore playing the shot outside of the line of your body. If you find you're overhitting, check your bat angle, it may need closing a little more. Equally, if you're hitting into the net too often, open the bat until you find just the right position. Of course, you will also need to make fine adjustments to your bat angle depending on the speed of the ball.

Building practice routines

You now have three strokes in your repertoire. Congratulations! In our experience this is more than many league players manage to develop in a lifetime—which is probably why they're still just struggling league players and nothing more. Let's take some time out to consider how you're going to develop and improve your game.

There are several practice routines you can use which involve just one stroke or combinations of two or more. It's important that you start piecing shots together as soon as possible because, after all, this is what a game situation is all about a series of differing shots played in succession with the combined strategic aim of winning the rally. As you become more proficient we have every confidence that you will soon be supplementing them with ideas of your own.

There are two ways of improving in any racket sport: one is by competition, in matches and tournaments, and the other is by practice. Although the latter may sometimes lack the glory and excitement of the former, you will soon discover that it's essential to fulfilling your true potential.

Forehand push

It's fair to say that so far we have talked about the pushing strokes in terms of them being safety strokes shots that give nothing away but at the same time gain very little. Don't be misled into thinking that they are somehow unimportant. There are certain, balls where the only option available to you is to push, and if you can't keep it tight the result will inevitably be that you find yourself picking the ball up off the floor because it's just been smashed past you.

In many respects, the forehand push is probably the most awkward of the basic strokes to master but for the reasons we have just outlined you would be well advised to persevere and conquer it.

Assume the same sort of stance as you would for the forehand drive, slightly sideways-on with your left foot leading your right. Because it's a pushing stroke you will need an open bat not too open, just slightly off the vertical. Make sure that there's ample space between your elbow joint which should be at about ninety degrees and your upper body. A common mistake made by many players is that they tend to cramp the shot because their body gets in the way of their elbow movement. Now, with your head near to the bounce of the ball, move your bat forwards from the elbow and slightly downwards at the same time. You should be making contact at, you've guessed it, the peak of the bounce. To help you co-ordinate the stroke, you can use your free arm to point at the ball just as you might use a gunsight. Your follow-through should be short and the stroke should finish almost as soon as you've hit the ball.

Try to resist the temptation to scoop the ball. You can avoid this by making a point of letting the bottom edge of your bat scrape lightly against the table surface. If the ball is short, stick your right foot under the table to bring your upper body and bat arm closer to its bounce. In this way, you will be keeping maximum control over the whole process.

Movement—and—footwork

One of the most important aspects of play, helping you join the various strokes together, is footwork. You may have the most beautiful technique in the game but if you can't get around the table without falling over your feet, it will all be academic.

To cover ground when close up to the table and to be able to react quickly, most players use what we term 'stepping footwork'. This is characterized by the fact that the feet do not cross over one another. It's a sideways skipping or even a shuffling motion designed to leave you with the right stance—one where your feet will be as wide apart as your shoulders and your weight will be centred on the balls of your feet.

Crossing your feet when up to the table can be suicidal. Once crossed, you discover that your body has become immovably entrenched, sideways-on, making quick recovery to the opposite wing almost impossible, Sideways-stepping keeps you square and, as you will have discovered by now, for most shots this is how you need to be positioned. Away from the table, when you're scrambling around with your back to the ropes, it's a different story. It is very difficult to move quickly without crossing the feet. However, because there is so much more distance between yourself and the table, there is also that little bit of extra time. You can afford, therefore, to run to the ball and this will obviously involve you in crossing your legs.

There are no definite and absolute rules about footwork and we are wary of coaches who preach along the lines of 'never' and I always. The reason being that we have been proved wrong so many times in the past. There are numerous examples of top-class players whose footwork at first sight appears to be a mess. But then, when you make a closer inspection, you discover that although their patterns may be unorthodox, they serve the player well without impeding mobility.

How good is your footwork?

Let's take a typical situation which crops tip during the course of most rallies. The ball is switched from your backhand, wide over your forehand. Your response is to shuffle lightly across using stepping footwork, of course and while retaining a firm base, you reposition your right foot so that it trails your left slightly. Your body weight is balanced over to your right leg. You are now in the classic position, ready to execute a devasting forehand drive. But wait a second! All this sounds too easy. This is what should be happening, but does it always turn out like this? How do we make sure that it does?

The answer lies in a technique known as irregular footwork exercises, But before we 'can go on to look at at this technique in detail, we need to look firstly at its counterpart, regular footwork exercises'.

Regular footwork exercises

Put quite simply, a regular footwork exercise is a practise sequence in which the direction of the ball is varied but the receiving player knows where. For example, in a repeat sequence of two balls down the backhand, two to the centre and then wide over to the forehand. Because you know in advance when the changes in direction are going to occur, the footwork pattern you need to adopt to return each ball is comparatively easy to perform and establish. The predetermined nature of the exercise lets you groove the pattern into your subconscious to the extent that it becomes virtually automatic. Well, this is the theory anyway. We can test it, and whether you can now react to this situation automatically, by using an 'irregular footwork exercise'.

Irregular footwork exercise

Irregular footwork exercises are a good way of recreating the rigours and uncertainty of matchplay. As you know, when you become involved in a game situation, the opponent will persist in that nasty habit of playing the ball to all parts of the table. And what's more, he doesn't even have the common decency to tell you where he's going to play each shot. An irregular footwork exercise should confirm whether your regular footwork patterns have invaded and established themselves in your subconscious.

A typical irregular footwork exercise would be one where the ball is played predominantly across the backhand diagonal, but your practice partner is allowed to switch one without warning down your forehand side. Try it, Did your feet move without you having to ask them or are you finding that you're still 'late for the bus'? If it seems that you're failing to get there quick enough, check that you are not just 'ballwatching'. Start 'batwatching' as well, and give yourself a headstart. Remember, anticipation might be the key that takes you out of the ordinary and into the extraordinary.

On the other hand, your apparently slow reactions may be attributable to your having rushed your development. You may have tried to master irregular practices without having first devoted enough time to more straightforward regular routines.

Recovery

There is a further factor which can help you make maximum use of both your footwork and anticipation. It is the position at the table to which you recover immediately after you've played the shot. Of course, this will depend almost entirely on the area to which you have chosen to hit the ball and therefore the target area on your side of the table which becomes available to your opponent.

It sounds complicated, doesn't it, but really it's all a matter of common sense. You can see how the position and direction of the ball you have just played fixes the parameters of the target area now open to your opponent. Your aim should be to reduce the opponent's scope, wherever possible, and then recover to a position which is just to the left of or central to his available angle of play. From this position, you should then be able to get to any ball he chooses to play Too far over to the left of the available angle and you will be leaving yourself exposed on the forehand side. Too far over to the right and you could be stretched on your backhand. For some players, an appreciation of this principle may already exist because they are gifted, instinctive tacticians, If you don't fall into this category, it means that you have one more good habit to nick up on the tricky road to success.

Service—and—receive

Table tennis is a sport littered with unfulfilled players who could quite easily put five points on their game if they devoted more time and attention to their service technique. In tennis, it is speed and power that gives the opponent his greatest difficulties in returning the serve. In table tennis it is the more gentle but no less threatening qualities of spin ' length and disguise which blend together to apply the pressure.

But you will only become a master of the art of service because that is what it has become, almost an art form if you are prepared to practise and work hard at it. Look upon service practise as an investment that pays handsome dividends well in excess of the normal market rate. All those matches that you've been losing 2118 or 2119 could be turned the other way. Before you read on and learn how to acquire a good service technique, it may be worthwhile first checking that you aren't in breach of any of the rules in this particular area. In the chapter 'The Game A Guide' you will find a short section which covers the various service laws and this should help to refresh your memory.

How to achieve a good service

In today's game, the type of service favoured by most top players is the 'two-bounce serve'. Essentially a short service, it takes its name from the fact that if the ball were allowed to continue its course, it would bounce twice on the receiver's side before falling away off the table. Ideally, the second bounce should occur on or about the receiver's baseline.

There are several reasons why this sort of serve has become so tactically advantageous:

1. It is difficult for the opponent to push it back short and therefore keep the ball tight.
2. If the opponent does happen to push it long or even flick the ball, the target angle available is comparatively small. This leaves you as the server with a little extra time to anticipate the direction of the return.
3. The opponent is often caught in two minds, Is it long enough for an attacking topspin shot to be attempted or is it too short and should it be pushed?

And if they do decide to push it, you should have been able to impart enough spin on the ball in the first place to make it difficult to control. Irrespective of whether you serve using your forehand or backhand, this type of service is achieved by following a few straightforward but relatively basic ground rules.

Firstly, make sure that the bounce on your own side of the table occurs midway between the baseline and the net. This means that the bounce on the opponent's side is also going to occur at the same midway point. This is the critical point which ensures that the hypothetical second bounce will then occur around the opponent's baseline. Secondly, to control the height of the bail's bounce, you should be striking the ball at a point during its descent which is roughly the same height as the net, around 15 cm or so.

Common sense tells you that to hit 1 ball at a higher point will only result in an unwanted 'bouncy' serve which inevitably invites the attention of the opponent's smash.

Thirdly, and this is where the real skill comes in, you need to keep your wrist loose to allow the bat to brush quickly across the ball to make it spin. We shall be looking at the whole question of spin very shortly, but it is a factor which takes on vital significance in the area of service and receive. Not only is it important that you are able to spin the ball, but your opponent must remain unaware throughout of the type of spin you have imparted and the ball's direction. In other words, you must acquire the skill of deception.

Lastly, as with any stroke, you need to recover and this should be part of the service action to the appropriate part of the table. Remember, we looked at recovery positions earlier as part of our examination of movement and footwork. If you choose to serve to, say, the opponent's forehand wing, the target area that opens up to him is your own forehand part of the table and vice-versa with the backhand.

The serving action

Let's return for a while to the service action itself. We mentioned how important it is to keep your wrist relaxed and fluid. If you want to spin the ball, your bat has to be travelling fast, but you must convert this speed away from hitting into the ball, because this will probably mean that it will miss the table altogether. On the other hand your aim is to slice or drag the bat face pendulum fashion across the ball's surface. With this technique, which requires a dexterity, touch and feel that it can take years to fully develop, the bulk of the energy exerted becomes transformed into spin with only very little being needed to propel the ball forwards.

One of the most popular service techniques favoured by many top players is the *high toss serve,* The most spectacular exponents are undoubtedly the Asian players who seem to regard the height of the roof as the only restriction on how high the ball is thrown. Twenty feet is by no means unusual and it is remarkable how well they control the fast accelerating descent of the ball and convert its speed into spin. From the opponent's point of view, this serve can be distracting and psychologically threatening. It looks fearsome and with skill it is possible to conceal the contact point of bat on ball with the free hand thereby disguising the type of spin which is being imparted.

We don't recommend that you necessarily spend the next six months trying to get to grips with this difficult service, You would be better advised on developing touch and feel on the ball with more modest services, with a consistent throw-up which is no more than a couple of feet in height at maximum, Try ·and I get into the habit of relaxing the wrist and elbow joint and synchronizing them together. An open bat angle with the bat brushing across the ball will help you to maintain control over the pace of the service.

On the backhand side, keeping the head over the point of contact will help you attain the control necessary. On the forehand side, check that your throw-up is not resulting in the ball lending too far away from the body so that you end up having to reach. Another good tip is to relax your grip and let the base of bat handle fall from the heel of your hand so that the bat is being controlled almost entirely by your thumb and forefinger.

Once you are able to generate an appreciable amount of spin, start to experiment with varying the point of contact of the ball upon the bat. Using the outer sections of the blade can have the effect of increasing the amount of spin because these are the fastest moving parts of the bat. The centre of the bat will produce slightly less spin. This is worth knowing if you want to disguise your service and deceive the opponent into thinking that the ball is spinning viciously. If you happen to be skilful enough to become a master of disguise, it will quickly become apparent that no spin at all is often as useful as spin itself.

The long service

So far we have concentrated our attention on achieving the two-bounce serve but there is undoubtedly a place in today's game for a low fast service—the long service. This clearly comes into its own when it is sprung on the receiver as a surprise. It's obviously important, therefore, that your body actions don't signal that a long serve is on its way. Your opponent should be kept guessing and it should only be at the moment immediately prior to contact that you adjust your serving action.

The main technical differences between the long and short services are as follows:

1. The ball should be struck about 10 cm or so above table height.
2. The bounce on your side of the table needs to be fairly near to the baseline, this will ensure that it bounces deep in the opponent's half of the table.

3. Your bat needs to move just as fast as it does in the two-bounce serve, except that the energy and speed you exert is directed through the ball rather than across it.

The best time to slip in a long serve is when you detect from the corner of your eye that the opponent is slightly out of position, A sudden change in pace and direction might succeed in generating a loose return which you can then capitalize on.

Receiving the service

A philosophy of just returning the service and hoping the opponent will make a mistake is a certain way to lose games. In many ways it might be a reflection of your general attitude of mind which should be positive and not negative, When you're receiving the serve, the stroke you play must be a positive one, which has a definite purpose in mind, At the very least, your aim is to cancel out the advantage which naturally lies with the server and restore the balance. Some people believe that the term positive' means that the ball has to be smashed out of sight, but this is entirely unnecessary.

Stance If your weight is on your heels what chance have you of moving quickly to the ball? Adopt a well-poised stance, facing the server with your bat pointing at the ball as it rests in the server's hand. As a general rule, position yourself in such a way that you can cover two-thirds of the table with your forehand and the rest with your backhand. Remember, though, that you might need to alter your position according to where the serve is coming from.

Watch the server's bat If he throws the ball twenty feet into the air, ignore it. Keep your eyes firmly focused on his bat throughout and try to detect the direction and type of spin on the ball.

Footwork Assuming the serve is short, move your nearest foot to the ball, keep your playing arm slightly bent and your head near to the ball for maximum control. There is nothing wrong with moving the furthest foot first. It certainly has the advantage of bringing the shoulders round but it can leave you a little exposed on your backhand. Moving the nearer foot is a shorter movement, is comparatively easy to execute and for most players often feels the most natural method.

Positive returns

What about the type of shot to use? Obviously, this will be a matter for your own intuition and judgment. It will also depend on the length of the serve but remember what we said about the need to be positive. Here are three positive returns to a short service which seem to be favoured by most leading players today:

Short push Using your wrist, take the ball at the peak of the bounce when it's at the same height as the net. Your bat should be slightly open and held comparatively loose to retain touch and control. Use the centre of the bat as the contact point and aim for within 30 cm or so of the net.

Fast attacking push Again, take the ball at the top of the bounce but use your elbow together with your wrist to push it deep and fast. Your contact point should be the edge of the bat and you should aim into the receiver's playing shoulder or, if he's off-guard, play it wide.

Flick With a closed bat face, hit over the back or top of the ball using your wrist, supplemented with a little elbow action as well. The contact point should be the edge of the bat.

Your wrist plays a critical role in all three of these returns. With the last two, it's especially important that you develop a technique which allows the bat to move quickly through the ball to counteract the effect of the server's spin.

Advanced techniques

To hit the ball hard or to spin it, you have to be able to generate power and speed of movement. You then need to be able to transmit this directly into the ball. If your basic technique is correct, this should be a comparatively straightforward process, If, on the other hand, you find that you're getting into difficulty, it may be that the foundations are not as strong as you thought. Running before you can walk is fraught with danger. Don't be afraid to 'return to go' and spend a little more time correcting a basic fault before you move on to the next stage.

Producing power

Table tennis is a 'whole body skill'. So far, we have concentrated on how the joints of the upper body become synchronized to produce the right striking action. When it comes to producing power for either spin or speed you need to be able to incorporate the joints and stronger muscle groups in your legs and lower abdomen as well. Then, you must be able to transfer your body weight into the ball. Probably the only way to illustrate this principle effectively is to look at two of the more widely used power shots that feature in today's game.

Fast forehand drive

This stroke is produced by accentuating many of the key features of the forehand drive. Start by making sure that your knees are bent a little more than they would be in the basic version, Your body weight should be supported predominantly by your back leg. Your upper body needs to turn to start the stroke from a more pronounced sideways-on position using your waist as a pivot. Lengthen your bat arm by increasing the angle at the elbow to around 120 degrees.

Start the stroke by pushing your weight forward from your right leg, through to your left. At the same time, your waist should be rotating to a position square to the line of play. This, in turn, will automatically start the process of drawing your bat arm forwards. Now, move your playing shoulder as well to increase the bat's speed. Finally, start to close your elbow and last of all your wrist. As with most attacking strokes, the timing point is the peak of the bounce. Make sure that your bat angle is such that you are hitting through the ball and not stroking or brushing it too much.

It all these joints have 'unlocked' themselves in the correct order your bat should now be moving like greased lightening! If it isn't, it could be that too much of your swing is taking the form of an elaborate follow-through. At least seventy per cent of the swing needs to occur before you get to the point of striking the ball and, most important of all, your bat needs to be accelerating at this point. There's nothing wrong with a follow-through it's an integral part of any stroke—but keep it economical.

Forehand kill

This stroke shares many of the characteristics of the

fast forehand drive, The major difference is explained by the word 'kill', implying that the rally should be dead once you have completed this dynamic shot. In technical terms, the transfer of weight from the back foot through to the front needs to be particularly emphatic if you are to hit the ball hard enough to produce the desired effect.

It is invariably used against a loose ball from the opponent one which has little speed or spin and tends to bounce about mid-table. Make sure that you start the stroke with your bat held at the same height as the bail or, if the ball is bouncing too high, at shoulder height at the very least. This is because your bat needs to be moving on a downward plane to prevent you from overhitting the other side of the table. To call he forehand kill a 'stroke' is a misnomer there should be no 'stroking' about it. All the energy and hatred you can muster must be transmitted straight through the ball.

Spin

An intuitive understanding of the effects of spin and how to handle it are essential to any devotee of modern table tennis. Being stroke with your bat held at the same height able to Impart fantastic amounts of spin upon the ball is without doubt a very useful weapon. However, it is just as important to understand the effects of spin and have the skill to read it, neutralize it and thereby deaden its impact. A failure to develop these latter skills is a characteristic of many aspiring players they might be able to dish it out but can they take it?

A table-tennis ball can be made to spin on its central axis by brushing the surface of the bat across it. For a split second the ball is gripped by the rubber and then rotated. This microsecond when this gripping effect occurs is often referred to as the 'dwell factor' or in some quarters 'the coefficient of friction'. Generally speaking, the stickier the rubber, the greater the dwell' factor arid in turn the gre'ater the spin that can produced.

A ball can be spun in any direction and this will be governed entirely by the direction in which the bat travels, Two types of spin tend to predominate in today's game: topspin, favoured by players with an attacking style, and backspin, preferred by defensive players. Sidespin is usually a hybrid version of these two forms of spin.

Topspin has the effect of making the ball dip downwards in its flight and then bounce suddenly forwards when it connects with the table surface, In tactical terms, the aim is to force a return which either misses the table completely or a loose, high ball which can be killed.

Backspin or *chop* is quite the opposite. If imparted correctly, it makes the ball hang in the air and stand up when it bounces. The common error made by most players dealing with backspin is to mistime the ball and, as a consequence, play it into the net. We will look at how backspin strokes are produced a little later. In the meantime, let's return to our theme of power and speed and in particular how they become important elements in the production of topspin.

Forehand topspin

A forehand topspin is produced in almost exactly the same way as the fast forehand drive. The source of power lies in the leg muscles which start the process of acceleration in the bat arm. However, the rotation of the waist, the use of the shoulder and the closing of the extended angle at the elbow are also part of the movement. It is just like moving up through the gears of a car:

1. First gear: the legs.
2. Second gear: the waist.
3. Third gear: the shoulder.
4. Fourth gear: the elbow.

However, unlike the forehand drive where you are largely hitting into and through the ball, the bat is instead brushed lightly against it. This means that your bat angle needs to be adjusted and the trajectory of your swing will be more upward than through about forty-five degrees to the floor. The faster you can move the bat, the faster you can make the ball spin.

It all sounds so easy when you read about it in a book but it's a different story in practice. The initial tendency of most players when they start out is to make the mistake of hitting the ball too much and not brushing it instead. Don't worry, this brushing action will eventually come to you. A useful tip is to keep your wrist fluid and relaxed in order to heighten your feel for the ball. At the crucial point of contact let the energy you have generated pass through your wrist, into the bat and onto the ball.

Fast and slow topspin

Many coaches talk in terms of fast and slow topspin. This can often become confusing because the descriptions 'fast' and 'slow' do not necessarily refer to the speed of the spin but usually to the speed of the ball, As we have already seen, power can be used for two purposes. One is for hitting the ball hard and thereby making it move rapidly through the air. Alternatively, it can be developed into making the ball spin. If we were to examine any given shot, we would probably find evidence of the two speed and spin combined together. Some of the energy you have produced will have gone into generating speed and propelling the ball forwards; the remainder will have gone into spin. The balance between the two will vary according to the manner in which you choose to strike the ball. The more you hit through the ball the faster it will travel, the more you brush the ball, the greater it will spin.

The amount of spin you produce can be increased by brushing up the back part of the ball. With a more open bat angle this will have the effect of pronouncing the 'loop' in the ball's flight, In fact, it's quite common to hear of players using the nickname 'loop' to describe this shot. A well-executed loop will make the ball kick violently forward and upwards on its bounce. As with all topspin variations, your lower body and legs play a critical part with your bat held at a near-vertical angle. Instead of pushing your weight forwards, push it upwards. This will help to ensure that you brush the back of according to the manner in which you the ball. Use this loop drive against choppers'—it can be a particularly effective method of combatting backspin, especially if you take the ball just after the peak of its bounce. In short, you will be capitalizing on the spin that's already on the ball and hopefully increasing it.

The fast forehand topspin is a different animal and

almost invariably used in different circumstances. The bat angle needs to be very closed and the point of contact is on the top part of the ball so this means that your weight is thrown forward with your swing brushing the ball on an almost horizontal plane. This stroke is a powerful attacking way of returning a topspin ball. It has become popular amongst many of today's leading players whose high level of skill enables them to play it fairly early in the bounce. The opponent is placed under even greater pressure because he has less time in which to prepare an adequate response.

Backhand topspin

Don't be misled into thinking that the backhand is somehow the poor relation as far as attacking spin shots go. Look at Andre Grubba of Poland or Andre Mazanov of Russia. Both are magnificent examples of players who can be equally as venomous on their backhands as their forehands. Anyway, if your opponent sees that you are incapable of opening the rally up on your backhand, that's precisely where he will concentrate his efforts. With the speed of today's game, the chances of compensating for a weak backhand by running round and using your forehand are remote.

It's not an easy stroke to master by any means. One of the main difficulties that most players encounter is generating sufficient speed to make the ball spin to and significant degree, The reason for this is that the playing arm is shorter on the backhand than on the forehand simply because the bat is being held across the body, It follows, therefore, that you must look for ways of widening the arc of your swing. One way of doing this is to make sure that you start the stroke with your bat held just below knee height. Keep your bat arm, and in particular your wrist, relaxed. To begin the stroke, bring your bat upwards in line with your body weigh' which is jettisoned in the same direction.

Contact should occur just to the left of centre of your stomach by brushing the back of the ball, at the peak of the bounce or just after. With this in mind, your bat angle should be slightly closed, just off the vertical, Although in most backhand strokes there should be hardly any rotation of the upper body, the backhand topspin, at very high levels of competition, is fine exception, if you're a right-hander, try turning slightly to the left and pointing to the bail with your playing shoulder. As you move through your swing, rotate your waist back to a position square to the line of play. This is another way of extending the arc of your swing and helping to increase the speed of the bat.

Chopping, floating, blocking and lobbing

To an outsider these phrases must seem meaningless to a table tennis player, they are part of the everyday vernacular, They complete the repertoire of strokes which form the technique of today's game. Not that any of them are recent innovations ' chopping', or the backspin style of play, has been around for donkey's years and was particularly popular in the bygone era of Victor Barna, Richard Bergman and Johnny Leach. 'Floating' is a variation of the chop and is essentially a chopped ball in disguise, a ball that looks as though it's been played with backspin on it but in fact has no spin at all, Blocking is the technique of countering fast attacking and topspin shots by taking the ball, half-volley fashion, straight off the bounce. Lobbing is quite the opposite, an away-from-the-table form of defence that involves lofting the ball high into the air, deep into the opponent's half of the table with plenty of topspin. Let's examine each one in a little more detail

Chopping Look upon chop or backspin in much the same way as topspin except in reverse. Instead of brushing up or over the ball, you brush down the back or even under i it. Whereas in the topspin game the power of I he lower body is vital, it is of less relevance to the chopper. Positioning and anticipation, coupled with a judicious use of elbow and wrist, sum up the major requirements of this technique.

On both wings, start the stroke with your bat held at about shoulder height, with an open angle just off the vertical. Your elbow should be at around ninety degrees and Your positioning should be a little away from the table. The timing point is just after the peak of the bounce and at about table height. On the backhand, stand fairly square I to the line of play but turn so your playing shoulder is pointing to the ball. Using your elbow, slide the bat down the back of the ball, brushing it outside your body but letting your shoulders rotate so that you finish square. You don't need much follow-through: as a guide, your elbow finishes the stroke not quite fully extended.

On the forehand wing, the same fundamental principles apply. Brush down the ball at about waist height, using a side-to-square stance but still rotating your shoulders so as to finish square, For good control, keep your head over the top of the ball as you strike it and try and transfer your weight through to your leading foot. This will help your recovery and leave you well poised for the next ball.

As with all strokes, there are no hard and fast rules governing the finer details of technique. Some 'choppers' play completely square because they find that a sideways-on approach leaves them vulnerable. By staying square throughout, it helps them move swiftly about the table, and switch between forehand and backhand with greater ease.

Floating To be a successful 'chopper', you have to be able to vary the amount of spin you impart. The more you brush underneath the ball, the greater the spin. To do this you will need to keep your wrist loose, letting it snap clean just as contact is about to occur. Equally, you need to be able to force errors by floating the ball at opportune moments, particularly against players who you know like to loop it.

Floating is essentially the knack of discreetly hitting the back of the ball as opposed to brushing it. In all the other respects, the stroke must look exactly the same as a normal chop and lure your opponent into thinking that it's loaded with spin. The skill lies in altering your striking action at the very last second just as you connect with the ball. This is achieved by a disguised adjustment of your bat angle to bring it almost vertical and by tapping the ball lightly so that it returns spinless. The follow-through completes the whole charade.

Chopping is often wrongly regarded as being defensive and negative. If all you end up doing is retrieving the ball with the same degree of spin every time and no variation you are hardly going to pose much of a threat. If, on the other hand, you can deceive and at the same time nip quickly into the table to kill any loose balls you will command far greater respect. There is nothing negative or predictable about the great choppers Chen Xin Hua or U Gun San, who are both quite capable of winning the world championship.

Blocking Blocking is simply letting the ball rebound off your bat on the half-volley. Hardly any forward momentum on your part should be necessary. Instead, you work off the speed and pace generated by your opponent.

Your approach to either the forehand or backhand block is the same as that adopted for the forehand and backhand drives. The main difference is that you take the ball as soon as it bounces with your bat angle suitably closed to contain the speed and spin on the ball. Other fine adjustments of the wrist can be made to vary the direction of your returns.

Blocking is all about feel, so keep your grip relaxed, and watch the ball and your opponents carefully to assess whether there is much topspin on it. Try to make your returns as deep as possible into the other half to cut down the angles of play available.

Informed opinion on the merits or otherwise of blocking as a worthwhile technique is divided. However, if you anticipate well and take the ball quickly enough it can be a remarkably effective way of limiting the amount of time the opponent has to prepare for his next shot. Often, it can be the only option available to you in dealing with a fast topspin ball and a good chance to manoeuvre him out of position.

Lobbing It's quite remarkable to see how some of the game's great players, in particular Yugoslavia's Surbek and France's Secretin, have turned what amounts to a last-resort shot for most players into a deliberate match-winning tactic.

A high bouncing lob, played deep into the table with plenty of topspin, is undoubtedly a hard customer to deal with. A miserable-looking, dead ball that bounces halfway, on the other hand, is useless and will almost always get the treatment it deserves. It's important that you give the ball plenty of height because this will buy you the time to regain a better position. Play the shot in much the same way as a high topspin with the aim of getting it as near to the opponent's baseline as possible.

6

BASIC FITNESS

Physical and mental skills can be inherited and each individual is different. So a coach must realise what a player is capable of and then select a suitable programme of training. Tests and measurements can deal with immediate objectives and the progress of individuals towards certain goals. When one evaluates, one is judging the amount of change in a player in a period of time. Although good physical and mental development will greatly assist the learning situation in table tennis it will not necessarily produce a great champion. The champion must practise 'hard on the table as well as off. For a table tennis player to function efficiently he must have organic and hereditary health, neuro-muscular coordination, strength and stability, emotional stability, social conscience, insight, attitudes, valued skills and morals,

When training players it is essential to measure all aspects of relevant fitness; find out the individual's weaknesses and then correct them. Before doing this, however, one must know exactly what type of fitness one wants to achieve. If a player can see himself improving physically it is a great psychological boost, and if he is training with his friends it can develop sound relationships and understanding of each other.

When a coach is testing players he should make sure the tests are reliable, objective and valid. The norms he uses should have been delineated from a large random sample of subjects.

Strength tests

When testing strength in a table tennis player it is important for the player to know why he is being tested. Many physiologists have shown that strength in an individual correlates with good performance in skills of a physical nature and that it is a big contribution towards total fitness. If a player is lacking in strength in relation to his size and weight, fatigue is more likely to occur and the peak of performance will be reduced. If one has good muscular development the body has every chance of functioning well and the development of new skills will be made easier. If one is feeling ill or is in a state of stress it is likely that strength will be affected.

To find a player's strength a good test is the Physical *Fitness Strength Index Test.* Over the past few years this test has had a reliability of 094.1 It is essential that the player is well warmed up before each activity and one should always allow him a practice to make sure he is performing the activity correctly. Always mark down the readings at the earliest opportunity and check that the player has not suffered any injury. The first test is for *lung capacity* and uses a wet spirometer. One should exhale slowly into the apparatus after deep inspiration. To ensure maximum exhalation the player should bend forward. After each player has used the equipment the mouthpiece should be washed in diluted disinfectant. The reading one is interested in, is the amount of air exhaled after a single breath. The second and third tests are for *right hand and left hand gripping strength.* For this test a manuometer should be used and the hand and arm should be abducted from the side of the body. Each hand is flexed in turn and the reading is taken on the manuometer to the nearest Pound,

The fourth test is for *back-lift strength* and a back and leg dynomometer is used and in the fifth test for *leg strength,* the same apparatus is used. Once again, in each test the reading 'is recorded to the nearest pound.

The sixth test is the pull up on the beams, using an overgrasp grip. If the pull up does not include a complete lowering and raising of the chin above the beam only half a count is awarded. This test is combined with the seventh test which is the *dip* to ascertain arm strength. This latter exercise should be performed on parallel bars and the subject should jump to a support position with the arms straight. It' he can lower the arm into a right-angled elbow position and push up again without his feet touching the floor, this will count as one repetition. If incorrect, half counts a re awarded.

Endurance tests

If one wants to find out a player's muscular endurance and cardiovascular fitness one can use the *Harvard Step Test.* This is a good test because it requires very simple equipment, no skill, and many people can be tested in a short time. It has a disadvantage in that some people are not fit enough to complete the test, so improvisation has to occur in the analysis of these people, A bench twenty inches high is used and players over eighteen years of age perform thirty steps per minute for five minutes and players under eighteen do thirty steps per minute for four minutes. Each step should be performed every two seconds and it involves rising onto the bench with the right foot, bringing the left foot up to join it then lowering the left foot to the ground and then bringing the right foot down. The back should be straight and the head pointed forward at all times during the test. If the speed cannot be maintained then the person is stopped and the number of seconds is recorded. The pulse reading should be recorded after one, two and three minutes after completion of the exercise and for thirty second periods.

Motor ability tests

If one wishes to test a player's motor ability there are various tests which can apply. Really one is trying to find out a person's immediate ability to play in a sport or event. Tests will include agility, power, hand-eye-feet coordination movements and strength. A simple set of tests are the *Western Motor Ability Tests.*

The player starts from a sitting position and two attempts at running the course are allowed. The fastest time will be recorded. This test can also be useful for assessing power and leg strength. The player jumps from a standing position with two feet together from behind a board and the distance is recorded from the back of the board to the heel of the trailing foot. The best of two tries is recorded.

The third test is for *hand-eye coordination* and it involves a person standing behind a line, six feet from a wall, and throwing a tennis ball underarm and catching it with the opposite hand. He then continues tile procedure so that each hand must throw the ball and each hand must catch the ball. He cannot throw the ball with the same hand all the time. The number of catches in thirty seconds should be recorded and there should always be a good supply of balls available and two trials should be allowed. One minute's practice should be allowed before the test and at no time during the test should the ball be supported by the body, or the feet move closer than six feet to the wall.

The fourth test gives a good indication of *upper body strength. An* area is marked out 75 ft long and 10 ft wide and after 25 ft the distance is marked out every foot. The player sits on the ground behind the starting line at the beginning of the court, with his legs straight and both feet on the ground. A basketball is held behind the head and it is thrown forward and the measurement is taken from the starting line to the place where the ball bounced.

The overall results are obtained on a percentage basis either within the group or better still by a set of norms which can be located in a standard book on tests and measurements in physical education.'

There are various methods of testing to assess a player's potential and his weaknesses but I will only outline a few more important tests. In the Vertical Jump Test an adjustable board with measurements in half inches is placed on a wall. The player stands with his feet flat on the floor, six inches from the wall, and with either his left or right shoulder at 90' to the board. He then straightens the arm nearest to the board, above his head and the board is adjusted so that the lowest point on it is at that height. The player then places a piece of chalk dust on his fingers, then jumps and tries to touch the board at the highest point possible. Three attempts are allowed and the best jump is recorded. This is a good test for assessing leg power and the distances jumped can vary considerably. If a player can jump more than twenty inches he is doing well. World-class high jumpers and basketball players have recorded jumps of over forty inches.

An elementary *Table Tennis Test* that is good for assessing motor ability was developed by Mott and Lockhart.' One half of the table is placed up against the wall with a 6-inch net above the table and against the wall. All that is required is to drop the ball onto the table and see how many times you can hit the ball above the net. Any number of bounces on the table is allowed and there is a time limit of thirty seconds. Practice is allowed before the test and the best of three attempts is recorded.

Basic fitness tests

Another group of fitness tests covering a wider spectrum of activities was developed by Fleishman. The first, a *Static Flexibility Test,* gives a good indication of the lateral flexion of a player. He stands with the centre of his back opposite to a wall chart that is at arm's length away from his body. Keeping his feet perfectly still and pointing away from the wall and with his hands together and the arms outstretched, he turns to the right and tries to touch the wall chart at the furthest point. He then repeats the exercise except this time he turns to the left. The degree of flexion in each turn is recorded from the chart to the nearest half inch.

The pre-session training period

At this time of the year physical conditioning is the

main priority in the training programmes. It provides a foundation of fitness upon which skill can be, based in the later stages of training. This stage of training is the most painful. The training load is designed to create the maximum peak for the year in an attempt not only to increase physical efficiency but, through tough and demanding effort, to set a new mental outlook to challenges that occur in the future. Usually only a limited amount of table tennis play is included in this phase of training.

The competitive period

During this stage of fitness training maximum load is gradually replaced by more table work. Weight training is reduced but is designed to create power. The number of circuit training sessions is lowered to allow more time for table practices. The long distance runs used to improve the capacity of the heart and to develop a psychological attitude, are altered to shorter distances covered faster. The training focus is gradually shifted from general physical conditioning to direct preparation for the forthcoming competition. This is done systematically to ensure that the Player can gain full benefit from the newly-achieved level of physical fitness by introducing more table training without allowing the fitness levels to drop. The wise planning of training during this stage has a decisive influence on the competitive performance.

Post-competitive period

This is the time after the last important tournament. Players should not stop training, as that would drastically reduce the acquired level of fitness, which should each year be higher than the previous year at the same point in the training cycle. To maintain fitness that has been acquired after the competitive season, flexibility exercises and active sports should be engaged in and time should be spent in correcting difficulties in techniques that were detected while playing in tournaments.

It is now usually accepted that to perform creditably at table tennis a player has to be dedicated, have adequate motivation and undergo a system of fitness training that is based on scientific principles. The basic components of fitness are strength, cardio-respiratory endurance, local muscular endurance, power, speed, agility, mobility, flexibility and balance. These attributes may be to a certain extent inborn but they have to be developed in a systematic manner based on principles of training which have evolved through time. The criterion of' skill combined with power is the most important aspect of fitness in which a table tennis player should excel but it is necessary to explain each component of fitness in some detail. Before dealing with the acquisition and the development of different physical qualities and the exercises which produce them, it is necessary to explain briefly how training improves physical fitness.

How the body functions

In its many forms, training is the means by which we try to accustom the body to an improved standard of performance. Training improves the efficiency of the body's various physiological systems muscular, respiratory, cardio-vascular, etc. so that they are able to function efficiently at the higher standard demanded of them. To understand how training methods effect this improvement we must first look at how the body functions.

During table tennis, striped or voluntary muscles cause the actual body movements. These muscles consist of thousands of long, dark- and light-coloured fibres bound together in bundles enclosed in sheaths. These are attached to bones by tendons and white fibrous tissue. When the muscles contract they shorten and pull the bones, thus moving parts of the body. Muscles, like all working things, require energy materials. We obtain these from some of the food we eat, in the form of glycogen and metabolised fat. Some glycogen is kept in the muscles for immediate use but most is kept in the body's storehouse the liver. When the body uses energy material, waste products are produced which, if left behind, would clog the muscles up. To break down these waste products the body uses oxygen, obtained from the air around us in another of the body's systems called the lungs. In fact, the lungs perform several functions: they obtain and supply air and they remove waste products, such as carbon dioxide, water and excess heat.

The body requires a transport system to deliver oxygen and glycogen to the muscles and to remove waste products This function is performed by the blood, which contains plasma to deliver nutrients, and red cells to deliver oxygen and remove carbon dioxide. Waste materials are also removed by the blood. Such a transport system needs a network of 'roads' along which to travel. These come in the form of connected tubes called arteries, along which the blood delivers energy material and oxygen, and veins along which it removes waste products.

Since the transport system uses fluids, some form of pump is needed to force it along the arteries and veins. The body's pump is the heart which is actually two pumps connected together. It, too, is made of muscle fibres, but of a more complicated type than the voluntary muscles used in body movement. The heart collects the blood containing waste products from the muscles and pumps it to the lungs. There the waste products are removed and replaced by oxygen. The heart then collects the blood again, this time from the lungs, and pumps it back to the muscles. Some blood is also sent to the liver to collect more energy materials. In this way there is a continuous supply of energy material and of oxygen, and a continuous removal of waste products so that they do not clog the muscle.

The development of stamina

Definition

According to Vaughan Thomas, stamina is defined as the 'ability to withstand fatigue'. For our purpose fatigue is anything which tends to cause a fall off in table tennis physical performance. According to Randall, Waine and Hicklin it is important to differentiate between an 'endurance which is mainly local in character and that which is dependent upon the cardiovascular-respiratory system.

Principles of training

Some of the principles of training suggested by Doherty include:

1. An endurance training programme should be developed that will improve physiological and mental qualities. The training should increase in a systematic manner.

2. In the early stages of' a training programme long distance running should be performed to improve stamina.
3. Careful progression in the degree of intensity of each training session should be undertaken to improve stamina.
4. Specialised aspects of a training programme should be introduced when a basic fitness level has been achieved. Therefore, table tennis players should develop those muscles that are specifically needed for their own style of game after they have achieved a broad foundation of fitness.
5. Every training programme should be developed specifically for each individual. It is important to consider what will be the best type of training to suit a player's emotions and social surroundings.
6. A player should always be aware of whether his training programme is developing endurance or strength. An endurance programme will improve the development of blood capillaries whereas a strength programme is more concerned with the development of muscle fibres.
7. A correct training programme for a group of people can be motivationally beneficial.
8. When the table tennis season has begun, a player's training programme should be designed to maintain rather than increase, his level of fitness.
9 Both general and specific fitness must be carefully planned throughout the whole year.
10. A training programme should be designed so that

it player is well prepared for important tournaments.

11. A well scheduled programme should be designed so that a player does not become bored.
12. A simple programme can be ail effective programme.

Specificity in training

Although the value of strength is no longer debated, this does not necessarily imply that we should go to the other extreme and develop massive strength only. Our first concern should be to ensure an all-round strengthening of the body. Selection of activities for strengthening work should be based on such criteria as:

1. Analysis of the movement involved in the particular stroke, in terms of type, speed, direction, etc.
2. Groups of muscles involved in these movements,
3. Sequence of movements, etc.

Special exercises designed to approximate as closely as possible to the same pattern and rate of movement, or part of the movement, should be performed, as this will bring into play the specific groups of muscles required for the particular event. In respect of strength training for any particular sport, like table tennis, it is important to be able to know:

1. The degree of strength required by the individual for championship performance.
2. The kind of strength required.
3. The time to be devoted to strength development.

4. The most effective method to be employed.

Methods of training for strength

Strength is essential in table tennis players, because it assists greatly in power. Certain muscles of the body need to be very strong so as to enable the weight of the body to be transported as effectively as possible. The thighs and the calf muscles need to be strong to move the body frame. The abdominals are an important factor in maintaining movement so as to ensure a good continuation in the build up, when playing a stroke. The racket arm is also very important, as it must travel as quickly and effectively as possible. This is not to say the trunk region is not important ' One must remember that in all sports and not just table tennis, force must travel through all areas of the body in a fluent manner so as to give maximum effect. If a certain muscle is weak and it is in a pathway of the direction of force it will not assist in the increase of force during its transference to the ball.

Weight training

An excellent way of developing strength is by weight training and with heavy weights and low repetitions. For each group of muscles involved one finds out ones maximum lift, then does X number of lifts at Y lb below tills weight. Then as the weight increases the number of repetitions will drop. Once a player has achieved two lifts at maximum weight, 5 lb Lire Lidded and a new maximum may be achieved. Strength training can also be developed with springs if no weights are available.

Any good weight training book will give many examples of different lifts, poundages and rest periods.

It is very important for a table tennis player to have strength and flexibility in his wrist, so that quick powerful movements call be made (especially for serving). Good exercises can be performed with dumb-bells for adduction, abduction, extension and flexion of' the wrist joint.

Isometrics

Professor E. A. Muller and Dr Hettinger of the Max Planck Institute, Dortmund, when investigating isometrics, developed a new type of' strength training. They reported that those people who did not have much time could achieve maximum training effect with only 40 to 50 per cent of application. The contractions were against a maximum load and held for a short duration. The muscle appears to be in it static state and may only be strengthened at the position at which the exercise occurs, This type of training seems to have little effect on dynamic strength or cardio-respiratory endurance.

One example of this type of training is arm and shoulder strengthening by pressing the hands together. The grip can be strengthened by trying to squeeze a hockey ball. The abdominals can be improved by attempting to lift wall bars with the feet.

Circuit training

One can plan a training programme to ernphasise the development of strength. One must concentrate on performing exercises where many repetitions are difficult and a maximum of' eight should not be exceeded. Examples can include weight lifting at stages in the circuit.

1. *Rope Climbs*
2. *Sit-ups* on an inclined bench.
3. *Half squats* with a weight that allows about six repetitions at the commencement of the course.
4. *Pull-ups.*
5. *Leg raising* with weighted shoes heavy enough to make six the maximum.
6. *Extending legs* against leg pressing machine where only six counts are possible.

Each time the exercise is performed it should include as many repetitions as possible. If a count reaches eight, then the task should be made more difficult by increasing the resistance.

front of them. When planning the curriculum of the course it is better to have a smooth continuity, with stages of progression in strokes, and not jump from one stroke to a completely different one, or the players' cycles of thought will be interrupted to a degree that is not beneficial for good learning. Therefore do not suddenly switch from a forehand counter attack to a backhand backspin and back to a forehand smash, but make the attacking strokes follow each other so that certain principles adhere to each of the two strokes, e.g. racket direction, weight transference.

When coaching a player who has formerly been coached by someone else, the coach should always be prepared to give a little extra time and patience. This is because that player may have been given certain stimuli which have resulted in grooved responses that need time for adaptation. Coaches should always make notes on players' interests so that if a particular player moves to another coach he can forward plenty of information which will help the player. This can be applied to specialised notes on training, consistency play, pressure play, free play etc.

A coach should always try to create an environment similar to the one which his players are likely to encounter in the next important event. It is useless for a coach to tell a player how to play an opponent on a slow Stiga table if he makes them practise on a Jacques table. It is essential that everything is as similar as possible if the best learning situations are to be created. When guiding players, it is essential that they learn for themselves and not just for fear of disapproval or desire for praise. Players will vary in response to rewards and punishments, the first being more effective. Neither, however, are as damaging as neglect. When a group of players is being coached and a particular player is never given attention, his attitude towards the coach will be poor, and this will create a poor learning situation. It is often the poorer player who needs encouragement and attention for progress to be made.

Learning depends on what makes a person want to work, and this often involves the reward and reinforcement theory. Psychologists have observed that if the reward acts as a 'satisfier', learning will be encouraged, while if it is an 'annoyer', learning will be discouraged. If a good player is rewarded for his success by tours abroad, he is likely to strive for greater playing perfection, but if his reward is only a little prize money for a tournament win, with no international recognition, he could be discouraged.

There are two types of reinforcement, negative and positive, and both play a part in progress in table tennis. A coach might say to his pupil, 'You will not play in the National Championships unless you win the area championships.' This is a negative type of reinforcement. On the other hand the coach could say, after a player has practised hard, 'I will enter you for the National Championships.' This is positive reinforcement. Players will respond in different ways to these different stimuli, so it is once again essential that a coach knows and understands the background of each player so that he can stimulate a player in the most effective way.

Psychologists have determined in the Problems of Arousal and Performance that the more people want something the more they will strive to get it. A table tennis player will really strive to achieve perfection in service technique if he knows that he has no chance of beating a player without it. This is provided the player really has the 'will to win'. He will try many variations of service strokes to obtain his goal, but in time mental and physical fatigue will set in and this will prevent the ideal situation for learning. Learning can be quite simply identified as drive, cue, response and reward.

Verbal praise by a coach can greatly assist learning in a player, but it is interesting how audience participation can affect a player as well. Psychologists have noted that when a player is involved in a relatively simple and well learned task, his performance is improved by' having someone watch him. If, however, a player is learning a new stroke, say a forehand topspin sidespin loop drive for example, then the presence of spectators may inhibit learning. Thus an audience impairs the acquisition of new responses and facilitates the performance of well-learned responses. This is why many players do not produce the same high standard of play in tournaments as in match play at the club. Many players are influenced by direct personal expressions of approval and disapproval such as nods, smiles, frowns and evaluative verbalisations. Players are constantly changing each other's behaviour through their deliberate or spontaneous reactions such as pleasure or displeasure, attention or inattention. This is why it is so important for team coaches and players to have the right psychological attitude to situations when one of their team is playing. A frown or lack of attention at the wrong time by the coach could be noticed by the competitor and this could set off an interaction which distracts concentration so the ideal situation for winning is lost.

When organising a table tennis programme one should always consider the facilities and equipment available, the ability of the players and the number of players involved. There are three main aspects of programme planning: The Syllabus, Schemes of Work and Session Planning.

The syllabus should cover all the varying potentials within the group and it should show briefly the type of work to be performed. One should always state an aim and the amount of time available for each session. One should divide it into main areas like warm-ups, consistency play, pressure play, fitness training, lectures and seminars.

When preparing a scheme of work one should always aim for a target of achievement within a set time. Naturally this will not always be reached, but definite targets should exist. Examples are backhand loop drives by X hours and forehand topspin sidespin loop drives by 'Y' hours, or improvement in strength, mobility or endurance within 'Z' hours. Always try to list tasks categorically. Always outline the skills involved in a certain stroke or exercise and explain how to coach them.

When planning a particular session which, for example, lasts ninety minutes, one should think carefully, with forethought and depth. A coach should always know the players' standard of work and he should then keep improving the quality of work performed. Within a session, always have an introduction, a main theme and a type of 'rundown'.

In the introduction always prepare the player for the more strenuous work that is to follow whether it be physiological or psychological. It is essential that a player's muscles shall be 'warmed', the blood circulating freely and the brain working thoughtfully with alertness. When trying to improve skills in a player, it is essential to give adequate time to developing awareness of limb positions and body coordination. It is always essential that there is a balance in training. One should always aim to give a reasonable amount of time to all aspects of the game. Playing continuously on the table without adequate physical training will not create the ideal buildup for competitive tournament play. It is essential that all players perform 'off the table' training for development of all-round muscular ability. If the training is not done, the players will not build up sufficient resistance to the onset of fatigue.

It is essential when coaching individuals or groups that interest be always maintained. This can often involve the personality and personal characteristics of the coach, and his ability to improvise, a quality which comes with insight and experience. One should always have the aims, objectives, and themes of a lesson clearly defined, and when one does this, it is essential that the coach knows the players' practical ability and physical performance. The ideal training camp should have six tables and twelve players. At international level 'two players to a table' should be essential and a group of eight should never be exceeded if only one coach is present. Any more than eight does not really allow an ideal situation for sufficient development and understanding between coach and player. When coaching one individual continuously, many pressures can develop between the player and coach due to their close relationship. They may see each other for many hours a day for many days a week and, although this is good for quick improvement, the coach will come into confrontation with the player more often. It is essential that the coach really knows the player's social life outside table tennis so he can be more prepared for the personality clashes which may occur. In a one to one situation each must have complete faith in each other. If this faith starts to wane the ideal learning situation will be lost.

In mass coaching always try to keep everyone involved as much as possible, If you have four players to a table and all the tables are being used yet many players are still inactive, you should have assistance from other coaches so they can give certain physical training activities, shadow play, lectures or seminars. It is preferable to have assistant coaches who can help you with advice if there are more than six tables with twelve players, or three tables with twelve players. Some type of rota system should be devised if groups are very large and players cannot be accommodated together. There should be a free period, training period and skill period. The players should be grouped by ability. I feel that if a girl is good enough to warrant a position in a men's group then she should be in it. Naturally, her physical training programme will need special consideration. During the sessions one should make sure that players play with others of fairly similar ability, but they should not play with the same person all the time.

Whether it is individual, group or mass coaching one should not extend consistency play for too long, otherwise mental fatigue could well occur before physical fatigue. One should not continue pressure training for too long or physical fatigue will affect performance.

Oranisation and presentation of researches, clinics, seminars and demonstrations

Researches

When doing research into improvement for table tennis players it is very necessary to consider the individual concerned. Every person has different attributes and deficiencies, whether they be physical or mental. One should not just look at one player's style and try to copy it. It is essential to look at a crosssection of styles and try to find the style of game which your particular pupil could benefit from. You must consider that it may be a good, idea to take different strokes from different players and introduce them to your player. Or you can model everything on one particular player, but one must always bear in mind the somatotyping of the person, and his physical capacity for work. Also his mental approach may make a certain style of game impossible.

It is essential to take films and video-tape of the best players if one hopes to model a game on their various skills. A big fault can be to watch someone and not realise the complexity of the movement, and without a film one will never be able to go over the full range of strokes effectively.

Clinics

Make sure you know the number of players involved, the number of tables available, the amount of time, and that there is a satisfactory supply of balls and nets. Always plan before the clinic so that everything will operate efficiently. Insist on the correct clothing and always be well aware of what the particular standard of play is. It is pointless planning a programme if it is far in advance, or below the ability of the performers. Try to play two to a table unless numbers necessitate four on one table. Plan the programme appropriately and remember to cater for the left-handed players. Always explain the programme for the day. Before each new activity explain what you want and preferably give a demonstration. Do not overindulge in excellent performance and exhibitionism, as this can lead to a feeling by the students that they have a 'bigheaded' coach. So the message is, never do too much demonstrating, but never do too little. At the end of the day always summarise and give constructive comments for future development.

Seminars

'These are very essential, but sometimes difficult to operate successfully. Much learning can be done by groups of people meeting and expressing ideas. One should avoid the formal approach if possible and concentrate on informality. This helps the pupils to express themselves in a relaxed manner. Always try to encourage all types of question, even if the individual thinks his question is foolish or simple. Often, supposedly foolish or simple questions turn out to be very important. Always try to assess each individual and try to find a way of making him participate in the discussions. It is often a good idea to ask people to prepare questions on a piece of paper before the seminar and then to read them out.

Demonstrations

Remember what has been said in talking about the

Clinic Stage: 'Not too much, not too little'. Always try to pick someone who can perform the demonstration if you cannot perform it yourself. It can often be difficult to teach points if no satisfactory demonstration is given and if this situation occurs regularly the pupils may begin to lose respect for the coach.

Recruitment development and talent identification

It is essential that a system exists within a country to ensure that any youngster from about ten years upwards has the opportunity to be considered for further coaching by Club, League, County or National level coaches. To do this a coaching system must exist where there is a nucleus, e.g. National Coaching Panel and a feeder system.

The national coaching committee

This can vary in size but an ideal number would appear to be about seven. The committee includes the Chairman, Secretary, National Coach, Staff Coaches and the Regional Advisers for the three areas of the country where National Coaches operate. Naturally they have a sound constitution and administration so that every member of the coaching profession knows exactly what is going on. A close liaison throughout the association is very necessary.

The national trainer coach

He is mainly concerned with the National Squads, concentrating on coaching, training and tours. It is essential that he attends all the major domestic tournaments so he can assess the lower-ranked players or any up-and-coming individual. He must also watch the different doubles combinations, as often the best singles players do not make the best doubles combinations.

National staff coaches

In England, National Staff Coaches are in charge of coaching for a certain area, e.g. North of England, West of England and Midlands, and South East England. It is essential that they, have close links with each other and with the National Coach and Panel. Their main function is to travel around the cities and towns in their area and organise sessions for players and Coaches, which may last from three hours to five days. They may be coaching basic skills to lower levels of performers or advanced ideas to the best players and coaches in their particular area. It is essential that they see what 'talent' exists in their area and then forward the best players on to national training camps where the best from different areas are coached. The coaches must know the standard of the players in other areas compared with their own because there may only be one from one area, yet six from another, who are worthy of further advanced coaching.

Three star coaches and trainer coaches

Three Star Coaches usually assist the area coaches at coaching sessions. They have almost the same qualifications but are not actually employed by the English Table Tennis Association. They also take courses for the area coach if courses clash. It is ideal to have one Three Star Coach in each county and for that person to operate as a talent scout and forward his potential players to the area courses.

Trainer coaches are rather specialised in that they are usually qualified in Physical Education as well as coaching to a high level on the table. They can be called on to take or assist any level of courses right up to National Teams.

Two star coaches

These coaches also assist in area coaching courses and will often conduct their own coaching sessions within a county. Usually they have a good understanding of all the leagues within the county and ask team captains and league secretaries to forward names of players who warrant extra coaching.

One star coaches

These coaches usually assist the Two Star coaches or, in certain counties where there are no Two Star coaches, they may run courses themselves. They also play in the league and look for potential players.

Club coaches

These usually come and assist in local league coaching, when leagues use their own initiative to help improve their players.

Teachers

It is essential that children learn to play in schools and that coaching courses are held to teach teachers how to coach table tennis. Usually their knowledge is very basic but their job is mainly to interest children and organise interschool leagues. They should aim to find a local club outside school which possesses a club coach, so progress in their players can be maintained.

This is briefly the coaching set up for the recruitment and development of players in England. The essential point to note is that there should always be an attempt for a close connection all the way from the bottom of the scheme to the top.

8

RULES AND REGULATIONS

Table Tennis, also called 'Ping-Pong' is a game patterned after tennis but is played indoors on a table. Simplicity of its rules and the fact that its equipment is so easily and cheaply available had made this game a most popular sport. Introduction of the hollow, featherlight, celluloid ball has completely revolutionised the game giving it new impetus, extra-ordinary speed and split-second precision. Studded rubber cash-mat on a ping-pong bat has added to its effective control of the ball and has made the game more fascinating.

Who first invented table tennis as it is played today is not known nor is the country to its origin quite definite. Britain, the United States of America, as well as India and South Africa have each been named as the birth place of this popular sport but most people concede that it began in England. Even those who suggest that table tennis was played first in India or South Africa agree that British army officers stationed there were probably responsible for its introduction into those countries. The game lost its appeal around 1904 and did not revive until after World War I when in 1921, the Ping-Pong Association was established in Britain. The name of the Association was subsequently changed to Table Tennis Association in 1926 and it became a World-wide governing Body. In 1933 the U.S. Table Tennis Association was formed as one of its affiliates. Japan, China, Hungary and Czechoslovakia have made especially strong showing in International play.

The table

The upper surface of the table, known as the 'playing surface' shall be rectangular, 2.74m long and 1.525 wide, and shall lie in a horizontal plane 76cm above the floor. The playing surface shall include the top edges of the table but not the sides of the table top below the edges. The playing surface may be of any material and shall yield a uniform bounce of about 23cm when a standard ball is dropped on to it from a height of 30cm.

The playing surface shall be uniformly dark coloured and matt, with a white line 2cm wide along each edge.

— The lines along the 2.74m edges shall be known as 'side lines'

— The lines along the 1.525m edges shall be known as end lines'

The playing a surface shall be divided into two equal 'courts' by a vertical net running parallel with the end lines, and shall be continuous over the whole area of each court.

For doubles,

— Each court shall be divided into two equal 'half courts' by a :white lines 3mm wide, known as the 'centre lines' running parallel with the side lines;

— the centre lines shall be regarded as part of the server 'right half court and of the receiver' right half court.

The net assembly

The net assembly shall consist of the net, its suspension and the supporting posts. The net shall be suspended by a cord attached at each end to an upright post 15.25cm high, the outside limits of the post being 15.25cm outside the side the line. The top of the net, along its whole length, shall be 15.25 above the playing surface. The bottom of the net, along its whole length, shall be as close as possible to the playing surface and the ends of the net shall be as close as possible to the supporting posts.

The ball

The ball shall be spherical, with a diameter of 38mm.

— The ball shall weigh 2.5 gm.

— The ball shall be made of celluloid or similar plastics material and shall be white or yellow, and matt.

The racket

The racket may be of any size, shape or weight but the blade shall be and rigid and shall be made of wood. At least 85% of the blade by thickness shall be or natural wood. An adhesive layer within the blade may be reinforced with fibrous material such as carbon fibre, glass fibre or compressed paper, but shall not be thicker than 7.5% of the total thickness or 0.35mm, whichever is the smaller.

A side of the blade used for striking the ball shall be covered with either ordinary pimpled rubber with pimples outwards having a total thickness including adhesive of not more than 2mm, or sandwich rubber with pimples inwards or outwards having a total thickness including adhesive of not more than 4mm.

— 'Ordinary pimpled rubber' is a single layer of non-cellular rubber, natural or synthetic, with pimples evenly distributed over its surface at a density of not less than 10/sq cm and not more than 50/sq cm.

— 'Sandwich rubber' is a single layer of cellular rubber covered with a single outer layer of ordinary pimpled rubber, the thickness or the pimpled rubber not being more than 2mm.

The covering material shall extended up to but not beyond the limits of the blade, except that the part nearest the handle and gripped by the fingers may be left uncovered or covered with any material and may be considered part of the handle. The blade, any layer within the blade and any layer of covering material or adhesive shall be continuous and of even thickness. The surface of the covering material on a side of the blade, or of a side of the blade if it is left uncovered, shall be uniformly dark-coloured and matt; any trimming round the edge of the blade shall be matt and no part of its shall be white. Slight deviations from continuity of surface or uniformity colour due to accidental damage, wear or fading may be allowed provided that they do not significantly change the characteristics of the surface. At the start of a match and whenever he changes his racket during a match a player shall show his opponent and the umpire the racket he is about to use and shall allow them to examine it.

Definitions

— A 'rally' is the period during which the ball is in play.

— A let is a rally of which the result is not scored.

— A point is rally of the result is scored.

— The racket hand is the hand carrying the racket.

— The free hand is the hand not carrying the racket.

— A player 'strikes' the ball if he touches it with his racket, held in the hand, or with his racket-hand below the wrist.

— A player 'volleys' the ball if he strikes it in play when it has not touched his court since last being struck by his opponent.

— A player "obstructs" the ball if he, or anything he wears or carries touches it in play when it has not passed over the table or an imaginary extension of his end line, not having touched his court since last being struck by his opponent.

— The "server" is the player due to strike the ball first in the rally.

— The "receiver" is the player due to strike the ball second in a rally.

— The "Umpire" is the person appointed to decide the result of each rally.

— Anything that a player wears or carriers' includes anything that he was wearing or carrying at start of the rally.

— The ball shall be regarded as passing 'over or around' the net if it passes under or outside the projection of the net assembly outside the table or if, in a return, it is struck after it has bounced back over the net.

A good service

Service shall begin with the ball resting on the palm of the free hand, which shall be stationary, open and flat, with fingers together and the thumb free. The free hand, while in contact with the ball in service, shall at all times be above the level of the playing surface. The whole of the racket shall be above the level of the playing surface from the last moment at which the ball is stationary on the palm of the free hand until the ball is struck in service. The server shall then project the ball upwards, by hand only and without imparting spin, so that it rises at least 16 cm. from the palm of the hand.

As the ball is falling from the highest point of its trajectory the server shall strike it so that:

— in singles, it touches first his court and then, passing directly over or around the net assembly, touches the receiver, court;

— in doubles, it touches first his right half-court and then, passing directly over or around the net assembly, touches the receiver, right half-court.

When the ball is struck in service, it shall be behind the end line of the server's court or an imaginary extension thereof, but not further back than the part of the server, body, other than his arm, head or leg, which is farthest from the net.

It is the responsibility of the player to serve so that the umpire or assistant umpire can see that he complies with the requirements for a good service. Except when an assistant umpire has been appointed, the umpire may, on the first occasion in match at which he has a doubt about the correctness of a player, service, interrupt play and warn the server without awarding a point. On any subsequent occasion in the same match at which the same player's service action is of doubtful correctness, for the same of for any other reason, the player shall not be given the benefit of the doubt and shall not lose a point.

Whenever there is a clear failure by the server to comply with the requirements for a good service no warning shall be given and he shall lose a point, on the first as on any other occasion. Exceptionally, strict observance of any particular requirements for a good service may be waived where the umpire is notified, before play begins, that compliance with that requirement is prevented by physical disability.

A Good Return

The ball, having been served or returned, shall be struck so that it passes over or around the net assembly and touches the opponent's court, either directly or after touching the net assembly.

The Order of Play

In singles, the server shall first make a good service, the receiver shall then make a good return and thereafter server and receiver alternately shall each make a good return.

In doubles, the server shall first make a good service, the receiver shall then make a good return, the partner of the server shall then make a good return, the partner of the receiver shall then make a good return and thereafter each player in turn in that sequence shall make a good return.

In Play

The ball shall be in play from the last moment at which it is stationary before being projected in service until it touches anything other than the playing surface the net assembly, the racket held in the hand or the racket hand below the wrist, or the rally is otherwise decided as a let or a point.

The rally shall be a let

— If in service the ball, in passing over or around the net assembly, touches it, provided the service is otherwise good or the ball is volleyed or obstructed by the receiver or his partner;

— if the service is delivered when, in the opinion of the umpire, the receiving player or pair is not ready, provided that neither the receiver nor his partner attempts to strike the ball;

— if, in the opinion of the umpire, failure to make a good service or a good return or otherwise to comply with the Laws is due to a disturbance outside the control of the player;

— if it is interrupted to correct an error in the order of service, receiving or ends;

— if it is interrupted to introduce the expedite system;

— if it is interrupted to warn a player that his service is of doubtful correctness or that he has failed to notify a change of racket;

— if the conditions of play are distributed in a way which, in the opinion of the umpire, is likely to affect the outcome of the rally.

Unless the rally is a let, a player shall lose a point

— if he fails to make a good service;

— if he fails to make a good return;

— if he volleys or obstructs the ball, except as provided.

— if he strikes the ball twice successively;

— if the ball touches his court twice successively;

— if he strikes the ball with a side of the racket blade whose surface does not comply with the requirements;

— if he, or anything he wears or carries, moves the playing surface while the ball is in play;

— if his free hand touches the playing surface while the ball is in play;

— if he, or anything he wears of carries, touches the net assembly while the ball in play;

— if, as he serves, he or his partner stamps his toot;

— if, in doubles, he strikes the ball out of the sequence established by the server and receiver;

— if, under the expedite system, he serves and the receiving player of thirteen successive good returns.

A game shall be won by the player or pair first scoring 21 points unless both players or pairs score 20 points, when the game shall be won by the players or pairs first scoring subsequently 2 points more than the opposing player or pair. A match shall consist of the best of three games or the best of five games.

Play shall be continuous throughout a match except that any player shall be entitled to claim an interval of not more than five minutes between the third and fourth games of a match and of not more than one minute between any other successive games of a match.

The choice of serving, receiving and ends

— The right to make first choice shall be decided by lot.

— The player or pair winning this right may

— choose to serve or to receive first, when the loser shall have the choice of ends;

— choose an end, when the loser shall have the choice of serving or receiving first;

— require the loser to make the first choice, when the winner shall have whichever choice is not made by the loser;

— in doubles, the pair having the right to serve first in each game shall decide which of them will do so;

— in the first game of a match, the opposing pair shall then decide which of them will receive first;

— in subsequent games of the match, the first receiver will be determined by the choice of server, as provided.

Organisation of Competitions

Provided the Constitution and Disciplinary Regulations are observed, any Association may organise and authorise open tournaments within its territory or may arrange international matches. The title events at one open tournament organised annually by each Association may be nominated as the Open International Championships of that Association.

International matches shall normally be regarded as friendly matches and not as championships, except for:

- World, Continental and other Regional Championships recognised by the ITTF;
- Continental Leagues, authorised by Continental Federations;
- Team competitions at Open International Championships;

Any Association may organise or authorise competitions within its territory and restricted to its members or to any group of them.

In an international restricted or invitation tournament, a player from an Association other than the Association in whose territory the tournament is held may take part only with the permission of his Association, unless general permission has been given by the ITTE or, where all the players concerned are from the same Continent, by the appropriate Continental Federation. No event may use a World title without the permission of the ITTF, nor a Continental title without the permission of the appropriate Continental Federation.

Representation

Representatives of all Associations whose players are entered in a World, Continental or Open International championships event shall be entitled to attend the draw. Representatives of all Associations whose players are taking part in a World, Continental or Open International Championships event shall be consulted on any alterations to the draw or any decisions of appeal that may directly affected their players.

A visiting Association shall be entitled to nominate at least one representative to the management committee of any international match in which it is taking part.

Entries

Entry Forms for Open International Championships shall be sent to all Associations not later than two calendar months before the start of the competition and not later than one month before the date for the close of entries.

All entries nominated by Associations for open tournaments shall be accepted but the organisers shall have power to allocate entries to a qualifying competition; in deciding this allocation the organisers shall take account of the relevant ITTF and Continental classification lists and of any ranking order of entries specified by the nominating Association.

The entry from for an open tournament shall specify the brand of table, the brand of net and the brand and colour of ball to be sued; the choice of equipment shall be as laid down by the Association in whose territory the tournament is held, selected from brands currently approved by the ITTE.

The entry form for an open tournament shall state the conditions of the competition and shall give details of any proposed deviation from the Laws and the Regulations for International Competitions.

Events

World, Continental and Open International Championships shall include men's singles, men's doubles, women's singles, women's doubles and mixed doubles title events and Open International Championships may also include junior, cadet and veteran title events. The recommended age limits for junior and cadet events are 17 and 14 respectively, the qualifying date being the day immediately before the start of the season in which the event takes place; for friendly matches the participating Associations may agree different age limits and qualifying dates. World and Continental Championship shall include 'men and women' team events, and international team competitions at Open International Championships may also be title events.

Team matches at Open International Championships shall be played according to either the Swaythling Cup or the Corbillon Cup procedure and the system chosen shall be stated in the entry form. Matches shall be determined by the best of three games in all events except individual singles proper, where they shall be determined by the best of five games.

Individual events proper shall be played on a knock-out basis, but team events and qualifying rounds of individual events may be played on either a knock-out or a group basis.

Groups

In a group competition, each member of the group shall play every other member of the group and the final order shall be determined by the ratio of wins to losses. (The ratio of wins to losses is calculated by dividing the number of wins by the number of losses). If two or more members of a group have won the same number of matches their relative positions shall be determined by considering successively the ratios of team matches won to team matches lost, of individual matches won to individual matches lost, of games won to games lost and of points won to points lost, as far as is necessary to resolve the order, and in these circumstances:

— only the results of matches between the members concerned shall be taken into account;

— if at any step in the calculation the position of a member can be uniquely determined with respect to the others, the results of matches in which that member took part shall be eliminated from any further calculations that are needed;

— if a member is eliminated from the calculation as provided in the positions of any remaining members shall be determined by reconsidering the ratio of wins to losses in accordance with the procedure specified.

Scheduling

In individual events in which each match is the best of five games a player shall not be required to play more than seven matches in one day nor more than three matches in any one period of four hours without his consent, except that in emergency a refusal to play may be overruled by the responsible management committee.

In a team event a team shall not be required to play more than three matches in a day without its captain's consent, except that in emergency a refusal to play may be overruled by the responsible management committee. It is recommend that, in competitions which include both team and individual events, the team events are planned to conclude before the beginning of any stage of the individual events which requires play by the team players; in World Championships; team matches may be held after the individual events have started only in emergency and with the permission of the jury.

It is recommended that, in World and Continental championships, one day free of play is scheduled during the Championships, preferably between the team and the individual events. The organising Association shall send to the Secretary-General and to the Secretary of the appropriate Continental Federation, as soon as possible after the end of the competition, details of the results, including points scores, of:

— International matches

— all rounds of Continental Championships and Open International Championships;

— the closing rounds of national Championships.

During World Championships, details of results including points scores shall be made available promptly to ITTF Officers, members of the Council and team captains; as soon as possible after the completion of the Championships the organising Association shall publish the complete results including points scores and circulate them to all Associations.

International Qualifications

The following regulations shall apply to all

international team competitions in which the team is representative of a whole Association, including the team competitions in World, Continental and other Regional Championships, Open International Championships and Continental leagues, but

— friendly international matches may be held under any qualification agreed between the participating Associations;

— other types of international team competition, such as international club competitions, may be played under any qualification agreed for the competition.

A player shall be qualified to represent an Association in a team match if he was born in the territory controlled by that Association or has been resident there for two years. When a player has represented an association he shall remain eligible to represent that Association unless he subsequently becomes eligible to represent another Association.

A player shall be regarded as having represented an Association if he has been nominated to represent it in a team event or a team match and has accepted such nomination, whether or not he plays. The date of representation shall be the date of nomination or the date of playing, whichever is the later.

A player who has represented an Association may subsequently represent another Association for which he is qualified provided that he has not represented his former Association during the previous two years, but a player may not represent different Associations in successive World Championships.

An Association may nominated to represent it a player who is qualified by birth or previous residence to do so but who is resident in a territory controlled by another Association provided that:

— he is in good standing with the Association controlling the territory in which he is resident;

— he is willing to accept such nomination;

— the Association controlling the territory in which he is resident is notified of the nomination.

An Association may nominate any player under its jurisdiction to enter any individual events for which he is eligible, except that a player qualified by birth or previous residence to represent another Association shall have the right to accept nomination by that Association. A player shall not represent an Association if he is under suspension or has been expelled by an Association having jurisdiction over him.

In World Championships, a player representing an Association for the first time shall provide, if so requested by the referee, proof of his eligibility to represent that Association.

Olympic Competitions

The Olympics Commission shall consist of the President, who shall be the Chairman, the Deputy President, the Treasurer, elected Continental representatives, a representative, a representative of the country organising the next Olympic Games and other members who may be co-opted.

The commission shall be responsible for:

- the planning, control and supervision of all table tennis events organised by the ITTF for amateur players;

- liaison with, as appropriate, the International Olympic Committee (IOC), National Olympic Committees (NOCs) and Associations on all matters concerning amateur play and Olympic competitions;
- enforcement of the eligibility regulations for amateur play and confirmation of the eligibility of entrants for amateur events;
- submission to the IOC of amendments to the eligibility regulations, as agreed by the BGM;
- drafting and submission to the BGM of proposals for a qualifying system for entry into Olympic events;
- appointment of a Jury, technical representatives and officials for the table tennis events;
- generally ensuring that the table tennis events at Olympic Games comply with the letter and the spirit of the Olympic Charter.

The Commission shall meet during the period of the BGM and at other times when convened by the President. The secretary-General shall attend all meetings of the Commission and shall draft its Minutes and Reports.

The Commission shall submit a written report to the BGM, and to the Council in the intervening years.

Amateur Eligibility

These regulations shall apply to all competitions which are restricted to amateur players, including in particular the table tennis events at the Olympic Games and any associated qualifying competitions. To be classified as an amateur and to be eligible for such competitions, a player shall not:

— be, or ever have been, a professional athlete or professional coach in any sport, or have entered into a contract to that end before the closure of any competition which he was entered as an amateur;

— have allowed his person, name, picture or sports performance to be used for advertising except under any contract for sponsorship or equipment which the ITTF or his Association or club has entered into, any payments under such contract being made to the organisation and not to the player;

— carry advertising material on his person or his clothing in any competition, other than trademarks on equipment or clothing as agreed by the ITTF;

— have accepted payment, benefit or allowance for playing except for

- prize money or participation fees at competitions specifically recognised by the ITTF, up to limits agreed by the ITTF;
- compensation authorised by his Association or NOC for financial loss resulting from his absence from work or other basic occupation in order to take part in any competition held under ITTF regulations, provided that in no circumstances shall the amount of compensation exceed the amount which the player would have earned in the same period;

Associations or clubs, at their discretion, may provide subventions to amateur players from the proceeds of contracts as described provided that

— not less that 15% of such proceeds is retained by the Association or club;

— subventions made to any player do not exceed amount sufficient to provide him with an appropriate standard of food, accommodation, transport, education and training.

The observation of the eligibility regulations shall be the responsibility of the Olympics Commission and the NOCs concerned, acting in accordance with the direction of the IOC Eligibility Commission.

Any case of infringement of the eligibility regulations shall be notified by the Olympics Commission or the NOC concerned to IOC, to be taken into consideration by its Eligibility Commission. A player accused of such an infringement shall have the right to request a hearing by the IOC executive Board, whose decision shall be final.

INDEX